The Ta... TransHERmation...

Once you become aware of who you are and who God called "you" to be, TransHermation will begin to take place. This powerful book provides spiritual redemptive insight on how to transform and improve your life. Lakeea Kelly gives a message of hope and healing to those who suffer with rejection.

Lakeea's willingness to help others through her transparency, exemplifies her bravery, courage, and determination to overcome adversity. I recommend this book to anyone seeking restoration, fulfillment and freedom from the oppression of life.

*~**Pastor Tina Lee**, New Harvest Christian Center, Battle Creek, MI*

I sincerely believe that the most significant call after salvation is transformation. When one is transformed by the power of God's Word, they take on a Kingdom perspective. This is the mindset that unlocks the victorious, purpose-driven, and fulfilling life.

Minister Lakeea Kelly has poured her heart into a literary work that details her life story, in a transparent, thought-provoking, and relevant way. Her real-life TransHERmation is the ideal model for women and girls everywhere who are seeking for greater!

*~**Dr. Kisia L. Coleman**, M.O.D.E.L. (Mentoring Our Daughters, Equipping Ladies) Ministries, Founder, Kingdom Church Int'l., Co-Founder, Chicago, IL*

i

TransHERmation indeed was transparent, raw, and real. This book was written beautifully, all the while sharing personal struggles and victories that will definitely help others with the issues that they face in life. TransHERmation encourages the reader, as well as brings hope to anyone who feels like they will never attain the goals they so deeply desire—both naturally and spiritually.

In TransHERmation, Lakeea shares her own personal steps on how you can succeed and overcome in your own journey. Upon completing this book, every reader will be ready to conquer whatever they are facing. No matter what stage of life you are in, you can believe that it's not too late for you to be Transformed!

*~**First Lady Freda Tolbert**, Freedom Faith Worship Center, Battle Creek, MI*

As Lakeea's mother, I found her book to be quite interesting. I experienced my motherly instincts rising when I read about some of the things she tried to sneak and do in her younger years. And, as I continued to read, I discovered many events happened that I never knew about. Some of them were so profound that I found it difficult to fathom all of what she experienced at such a young age; right down to the spirit of abandonment. I often asked what was troubling her, but she would always say she didn't know. It was heartbreaking and, as her mother, it made me feel helpless.

However, now, I am a living witness of how Lakeea has transformed from a broken child, to an awesome woman of God. She went from a happy little girl—who loved to play outside—to being a daddy's girl who loved her daddy endlessly. From a rebellious disobedient child, to a young woman who really didn't know at the time what she wanted to do; and to a young mother who went through a phase of depression. But then, as the years went by, I watched how God transformed her into a woman who loves the Lord, and began to walk and operate in her God-given purpose. It has been a journey, but I thank God for where He has brought her from, and for what He is doing in her life. I often think about how God has just changed her. It was nothing but God! We serve an awesome and an amazing God!

The title alone, "TransHERmation", is going to compel readers, especially women of all ages, to purchase the book. As you read TransHERmation, you will find it to be so interesting that it will be hard to put it down... you will just want to keep on reading it just to see what's next!

It reminds women that they are not alone in the things they face, especially those who are too ashamed to tell their story. They will learn that no matter what their situation is, there is always hope by putting their faith, trust and belief in God. First, you must love God enough to trust Him, and then you must love yourself enough to fight it through, never giving up... never listening to the devil's lies.

As Lakeea stated in her book, "It is the victorious story of my journey, from darkness to light, from brokenness to wholeness, and from captivity to freedom." And that too can be someone else's story. A life testimony! A God-inspired book on how God was in her life even at such a young age—how He transformed her from "brokenness to wholeness, and from captivity to freedom." That is powerful and life-changing!

~**Cynthia Little**, Certified Mentor & Coach,
Nashville, TN

Taheera
Wilson-Forbes,

May God continue
to Shine His face upon
you and shower you
with His love and blessings
in abundance! :)

love,
aunt
Kelly

How God Can Take Everything You've Been Through
and Transform You for His Glory!

Lakeea Kelly

TransHERmation - How God Can Take Everything You've Been Through and Transform You for His Glory!
by Lakeea Kelly

Cover design, editing, book layout and publishing services by KishKnows, Inc., Richton Park, Illinois, 708-252-DOIT admin@kishknows.com, www.kishknows.com

ISBN 978-0-692-93233-9
LCCN 2017912191

For permission requests, please contact Lakeea Kelly: lakeeakelly@gmail.com

Some Scripture references may be paraphrased versions or illustrative references of the author. Unless otherwise specified, all other references are from the New International Versions of the Bible.

Printed in the United States of America.

Dedication

To all the women who have experienced rejection, abandonment, depression and shame, this book is wholeheartedly dedicated to you. This woman has been through tremendous pain, heartaches, trials, tribulations, afflictions and difficult life situations, but she knows that she is not defined by what she has been through. She has multiple assignments and duties — Yes, she is meant to walk out more than one purpose and mission while here on Earth! — and that outweighs what she has endured. This woman is going on an endless TransHERmation that is causing her to move into her God-given gifts and talents.

Table of Contents

Introduction

Life was good. I was in my late twenties. There were no major issues, except for the everyday life ones that came along like paying bills, taking care of my children and going to my nine-to-five. I never fathomed that life would take a major shift. I never imagined that I would suffer from depression. It was a blow to my mind—as if I was on a battlefield all by myself; and I had several guns shooting straight at my head, causing me to spiral downwards into a deep depression...

It started with one thought; just a tiny seed of guilt and shame, and that seed took root—and grew, until it became bigger and bigger. I had been ready to completely surrender my life over to God; I had been ready to say "Yes." I had been ready to do His Will—but I was tormented by my past. I was plagued in my mind with the sin that I had committed before. I had even contemplated saying "Yes." It was as if I was in court, and the prosecutor was rendering me guilty, although I was proven innocent.

Day and night, my thoughts were filled with the memories and flashbacks of everything that I had done, and did wrong. I felt as if God was getting ready to punish me severely because I had denied Him so many times before. I felt as if I was not worthy of His forgiveness, His mercy or His kindness. I had the devil in my ears telling me that I was going to pay for the very thing that I had just asked forgiveness for, which was a lie—but I was starting to believe the lie. My mind was so clouded and confused, that I could not even begin to see the truth. I was terrified of being punished by God for committing sin. I cried so many tears that I could have filled up a whole bathtub.

I am a firm believer that depression first begins with a thought that the enemy plants in your mind. He will take one thought and magnify it until you are confused about who you are in Jesus Christ. His agenda is to bring you into such a dead state, that you are not able to identify with your purpose, or the prophetic words that have been spoken over your life. Depression clouds your understanding and perception of what God has already declared.

But like the sun breaking through and burning up the fog, God shone his light on me. Psalm 4:18, "The path of the righteous is like the morning sun, shining ever brighter till the full light of day." I had to literally fight for my life through the working of the Holy Spirit, with much endurance and perseverance, to come out of that state of depression.

This is my story—His story—of transformation, or as I like to declare it: TransHERmation. It is the story of God's faithfulness to complete the work that He began in me before I was born. It is the victorious story of my journey from darkness to light, from brokenness to wholeness, and from captivity to freedom.

My journey is not yet over, and I would like to invite you to travel with me through the pages of this book. The first part of this book is my life story, up to the turning point where I surrendered to God's Will for my life and began to journey closer with Him. This was the catalyst that sparked off the TransHERmation. The second part of the book contains the life lessons and truths that God has taught me as I have walked through my past with Him. The lessons that have shaped my TransHERmation.

My prayer is that as you work through this book, you too will experience TransHERmation inside and out, and find freedom in becoming the person that God has declared and willed you to be.

Now to him who is able to do immeasurably more
than all we ask or imagine,
according to his power that is at work within us,
to him be glory in the church
and in Christ Jesus throughout all generations,
or ever and ever!
Amen.
Ephesians 3:20-21

Chapter 1

Household Drama

The Younger Years

I grew up in a small town called Battle Creek in Michigan, in the middle of Chicago and Detroit. My neighborhood was considered to be the "hood" of Battle Creek.

I was not athletic or an honors student, or a kid that was recognized for great accomplishments. I grew up in a middle-class home; both of my parents worked decent full-time jobs.

I have a younger sister. We are about four years and nine months apart, so for a while, before she was born, I was the only child and was considered spoiled. All I heard was, "You are so spoiled." I didn't even know what spoiled meant, but since I was the only child, I probably was. I did not like the idea of my mom having a baby. I do remember, at the age of four, kicking my mom in the stomach and saying, "I don't like that baby!". I already had sibling jealousy before she even came into this world because I was no longer going to be the baby, and the only baby at that.

I loved playing outside like any other kid and had to be home when the streets lights came on. My mom would not allow me to go outside until noon, which seemed way too late to me. When I woke up at 8:00 a.m., it was time to go outside. I played all day. The only time I came in the house was to get something to drink. I was a tomboy; I skinned my knees every day, and I am not exaggerating.

1

One summer's day, when I was about four, I decided to put on some jeans because I was tired of skinning my knees. This time I was going to protect my knees. Everybody on my street knew why I was wearing jeans that day, even my neighbor said, "You're tired of skinning your knees every day, that's why you have on those jeans." Wearing those jeans didn't give me much justice; I just ended up with holes in my jeans with skinned knees. I must have been very clumsy as a child!

At the end of that summer, it was time for school to start. For some reason, I had this desperate need to start kindergarten. I begged my mom to let me go to school; she finally said yes. I was in kindergarten at the age of four. My mom walked me to school on my first day so that I could get used to the route. Back then, it was perfectly fine to walk to school by yourself, even at the age of four.

However, because she was working, for the rest of my first week of kindergarten, my daddy had to make sure I got off to school. Oh boy, that meant he had to comb my hair too! My mom had rolled my hair the night before, and told my dad that all he had to do was take the rollers out and comb my hair back and put it in a ponytail. Nope, Daddy did not know anything about combing hair—he took the rollers out and let my hair go! That was my first experience of being teased and made fun of as a school kid. The other kids talked about my hair so badly. To be exact, they said it looked like an old-lady hairstyle. They weren't lying, but I was so hurt. That day, I ran all the way home from school because I was so embarrassed about my hair—but Daddy had done the best he could do.

I was a daddy's girl. When Daddy would come home from work, I would get so excited and jump up and yell... "Daddyyy!" Daddy would play with me and tickle me all the time. That was his thing. He would grab me up and tickle me.

2

Daddy worked second shift so I didn't see him as much and I looked forward to spending time with him on the weekends. Spending time with him was one of my favorite things to do.

On the weekends, when Daddy would get ready to leave the house, I would always ask him if I could go with him. I wanted to be right there with my daddy. It didn't matter where he was going or what he was going to do, as long as I was right there. Daddy never said, "You can't go with me." It was always, "Come on.", and I would hop into his car. I always sat in the front seat on the armrest. In those days, it was not illegal to sit there and it was my favorite spot, right by Daddy.

We would often visit my uncles. My daddy and uncles were very close and they hung out together drinking, smoking and talking like the best of friends. At other times, my daddy would take me with him to his friends' houses and I would hang with him all night. It didn't matter to me, as long as I was with my daddy. There were also plenty of times when my dad would take me drag racing with him. For those that don't know what it is, drag racing is when you race your car on country roads or even on the highway against other cars. This is dangerous and if my mom had known, she wouldn't have been happy.

However, I couldn't be around everything he did. Sometimes he would drop me off at my grandma's house. I enjoyed going over to Grandma's house to play with my cousins. Plus, all he had to do was give me a dollar so that I could walk to Cady's, the neighborhood store, with my cousin, and buy a bag full of penny-and-dime candy.

Boy, did my cousins and I have fun at Grandma's house. We were creative and knew how to have fun. We didn't have cell phones and all this technology stuff that we have today. Those were the days—riding my bike all around the neighborhood, being daring, and jumping off the railroad tracks with my bike, making mud pies, running around in the woods, playing hide-and-seek, playing 'house' with the other kids in the neighborhood and playing instruments made out of cans.

The Reality

So far, it sounds like I grew up in a pretty normal home, except for the times when my dad would drag race late at night, and I would be the only little kid on the scene, sitting in the back seat.

However, there were plenty of nights when Daddy stayed out really late, way past the time he would finish work. There would be no phone call or message. He would just come in when he was ready. This caused a lot of issues with my mom. When my mom would confront him, he would get irate and verbally abusive. But— it didn't stop with the verbal abuse—he would then get physical with my mom.

It seemed like almost every night, I heard and saw my dad verbally and physically abuse my mom. I remember being a little girl, running back and forth from room to room, crying and screaming—hoping it would get my dad's attention enough for him to stop. It didn't. It was as if I wasn't even there.

My dad was very temperamental, which explained why I had numerous temper tantrums as a little girl, right into my teenage years, and even as an adult. The seed of anger was planted in me from a very early age. I will talk more about this later on in the book.

Like any other kid, I didn't want to see my parents fighting, but it became a "normal" part of our household. I would go to school every day and be a normal kid that enjoyed being outside and playing. But at night, I would witness my mom going through tremendous abuse, and I would hear words that a child shouldn't hear any parent say. It wasn't something that I talked about because, as I stated, it was "normal" for my life. And who would want to go around broadcasting that they witness their mom being abused on a consistent basis? Something like that is too shameful and embarrassing to admit.

One night, I wanted to go over to my grandma's house, but I was also scared to leave my mom home alone, because I feared my dad was going to hurt her. Well, my fears were valid. My mom ended up with a torn ligament leg and put on crutches. I began to hurt so badly for my mom. My mom is one of the strongest women I know. She could write her own book with everything she has been through; maybe one day she will. One of the most memorable traumas was when my dad locked us out of the house. I believe he was extremely angry with my mom. My mom was determined to get in and smashed the glass window on the door with her bare hand. That was a demonstration of bravery to me; she was not going to let her daughters be out in the cold for nobody!

When I was seven years old, my mom reached her breaking point. She could no longer take it. She sat me down and let me know that she was divorcing my dad. At the time, I was okay with my mom divorcing him and us going to live with my grandmother, because I knew my dad was abusive and I didn't like my mom going through all that pain. I would say, at that young age, I had a lot of wisdom. Most children do not want to see their parents split, but I was all for it! Plus, I was a grammie's girl, and loved the idea of being at Grammie's house 24/7.

Daddy's World—Daddy's Girl

Although my father was the way he was, I loved him dearly and never had a bad word to say about my daddy. If I heard someone say something about my dad that was out of line, I would defend him in a minute. In my eyes, that was my daddy and that was all that mattered. You had better not say anything bad about him, or you had to deal with me!

When my daddy and mom divorced, it was as if he divorced my sister and me too. We didn't get any calls on Christmas, our birthdays, or for that matter, any other day. There were times that I would see my dad in the streets, and he would ride by and honk as if he had just seen one of his homies. He was probably working or busy, but that was how I felt, and even if he was busy, it was still no excuse. My thinking was—*I haven't seen you in I don't know when, and all I get is a honk and a wave*—but that was how it was and I just accepted it. I didn't know that the abandonment and rejection, and consequent hurt and anger, would bring in a harvest much later on in my life.

Sometimes, with a little liquor in his system, Daddy would muster up enough nerve to call my grammie's house. It wasn't about talking to us—it was about talking to my mom. Sometimes I would get a kick out of it because he was trying to get his mack on. It was obvious he still had a thing for my mom.

Years later, it was revealed to me that my dad was on drugs. I couldn't and didn't believe it. I wanted proof! I didn't even understand what drugs were at that time.

Well, one summer when I was about sixteen, I was given that proof. My sister and I went to stay with my daddy that summer. We were chilling around the apartment and nothing seemed unusual about that particular evening, until I went upstairs and my daddy called me.

6

I went into the bedroom and there was Daddy with a glass drug pipe in his mouth. He called me over to him and he blew the smoke in my face, and gestured to me to join him. I was totally stunned; I couldn't believe that my daddy would even consider offering me drugs!

When I first heard that Daddy had a drug problem, I didn't want to believe it. Now that I had seen it with my own eyes, I was devastated and heartbroken to the core. That night, I curled up in the bed and cried for hours. There was so much pain bottled up in me from this incident that I was disgusted with him for a long time. I poured out my heart in writing to help me work through this heartache. I later asked him, "Why did you do that?" and he said it was because he wanted to make sure I didn't get hooked on drugs. That did not make any sense at all!

However, I didn't and couldn't hold a grudge against my dad forever. As I already stated, nothing could persuade me from not loving my dad. It seemed as if after that first incident of me witnessing him on drugs, he became more comfortable doing drugs in front of me. It was nothing for him to come out of the room smoking the drug pipe. I resented him for doing that. Although it was no longer a secret that he was doing drugs, I did not want to see it.

Later on, when I started smoking weed (we'll talk more about this later on the book), Daddy pretty much opened the door for me to smoke around him if I wanted to. His thing was, "I rather you do it at home where I know you are safe, than in the streets" However, I still honored my dad better than that; I couldn't bring myself to smoke weed in the same house with him.

As I grew older, despite all the wounds and hurt, my love still remained. I was the oldest, and I pretty much had that oldest-sibling mentality; I was going to be there to honor my dad and be there for him no matter what.

I would visit him every now and then, and would call him up. I can remember calling him on one of my birthdays, and him saying, "I was waiting on you to call me." I thought that was so comical... Really?... You are waiting on me to call you on MY birthday? But that was my daddy, so it didn't faze me because I had grown used to him disappointing me—or so I thought, until much later on in life when God started dealing with me and revealed the deep hurt and abandonment.

During the times that I would see my dad, he was an easy person to talk to. He kept it real and often talked to me about his struggles. I respected my dad for keeping it real with me and not sugarcoating stuff; I can definitely say he was not a phony. I responded very well to him keeping it one hundred percent.

I am that way to this day. I have a respect and admiration for those that keep it real and do not put on a façade, and act like something they are not, or act one way in person, but another way behind closed doors. Not to say that everyone's "keeping it real" is acceptable, but they take the guess work out of wondering who or what they are.

The Bible talks about being either hot or cold. Even God has a better respect for a person that is honest and has integrity, versus a hypocrite; a person pretending to be something they are not. Hypocrites are great actors and actresses.

Ezekiel 33:31-32 says, "My people come to you, as they usually do, and sit before you to hear your words, but they do not put them into practice. Their mouths speak of love, but their hearts are greedy for unjust gain. Indeed, to them you are nothing more than one who sings love songs with a beautiful voice and plays an instrument well, for they hear your words but do not put them into practice."

That verse describes a hypocrite. Their mouths speak love, but their hearts are filled with evil. Daddy was no hypocrite. I can remember my dad saying, "I may not be nothing (he used a different word), but my kids are." He often told me, that a day didn't go by where he didn't think about his kids.

My dad is no longer living. I do believe he accepted Jesus Christ in the hospital. He wanted Jesus; he wanted something different, but just didn't know how. I remember Daddy saying, "I try to read the Bible, but I just don't understand." I remember him saying, "I want to change, but I don't know how." God used me as his intercessor to lead him to Jesus Christ when he was on his deathbed.

Grammie's House

Let me take you back to the time when we moved in to live with Grammie when I was seven years old. Life staying at Grammie's house was smooth sailing. My grammie was one of the nicest people you could meet. She made everyone feel welcome and she had a kind heart. I saw Jesus in my grandmother.

She would read her Bible and pray every night, and as a young child, when I spent the night with her, I would be right there with her when she prayed and read her Bible. After seeing her read the Bible so much, I decided I would try to read the Bible too, but there were so many *"ye's"* and *"thou's"* that I put it down. I remember thinking, *"How does Grammie even understand what the Bible is saying?"* It was at Grammie's that the tiny seeds of faith were planted.

Since we were now living at my grandmother's house, we started attending church. My mom only made my sister and I attend Sunday school; we didn't have to sit in the regular service, unless she was running late for church and didn't have time to drop us off back home. I dreaded those days when we had to stay at the regular service because it was so dead and boring; no life or power at all! We didn't attend the same church as my grandmother, but I would sometimes go with her and preferred her church because I felt they were livelier. *"At least they sing a little more upbeat hymn songs than the boring ones!"* Those were the types of thoughts that I had about her church.

Staying with Grammie brought peace and stability into our lives; there was no more arguing and fighting at night. The only yelling going on was me getting into trouble because I did something that my mom clearly told me not to do.

As time went on, I began to get resentful towards my mom for the divorce. It was as if I started being affected emotionally by the divorce, and I started to blame her. I became rebellious and disobedient. I was quite a hard-headed child. My mom would tell me not to do something; and as soon as she was out of my sight, I was doing that very thing. I guess you could say between my sister and I—I was the problem child.

My grandmother was my defender. I could be clearly deserving of a scolding or whooping, but my grandmother would always, and I mean always, interfere to stop my mom. Once, she chased my mom around the house, while my mom was chasing me to give me a spanking. Grammie was not going to let my mom spank me; too funny! I would always get tickled because it was, "Grammie to the rescue!" I was very close to my grandmother. I was with her a lot and we went on plenty of shopping trips together, and our favorite restaurants were Mr. Don's and Big Boy. I never got tired of being with my grandmother; plus, she spoiled me, which I loved. Her "no" always turned into a "yes".

Life seemed to be quite steady at Grammie's house, until my mom met this military man. I gave any man my mom dated a hard time because he was not my daddy. I didn't know this military man, and didn't want to know him. I did not like him at all. All I knew was—he was not my daddy.

Things started moving fast with this military man, and one day, my mom told me that they were getting married. *"Married?!"* I couldn't understand what she saw in this guy. I wanted to convince my mom not to marry this man. Who was he anyway? He talked fast and had a down-south accent. I made it very clear to him that he didn't have a chance in winning me over. My favorite line was, "You are not my daddy."

Not too long after my mom told us that she was getting married, she announced that we were moving to Germany. I was in the fourth grade in elementary school. I had a pretty good social life with my friends; I was close to my family and life was good with Grammie.

I became very angry. I literally had temper tantrums and outbursts about moving—I did not want to move. But, as you know, a child does not determine and decide what he or she is going to do. It was time for us to move, not to another neighborhood, city or even another state, but out of the country—to Germany.

Chapter 2

Life Overseas: The Birth of Hurt and Bitterness

To everything there is a season,
and a time to every purpose under the heaven:
A time to be born, and a time to die;
a time to plant, and a time to pluck up
that which is planted;
Ecclesiastes 3:1-2 (*King James Version*)

Seasons Change

Off to Vilseck, Germany we went, from nine to eleven years old. Most people would say that having the chance to live in Germany is an opportunity of a lifetime. I did not see it that way. I was very angry to be moving to Germany. It was too far away, out of the country. You couldn't just get in the car to see your family. You couldn't even pick up the telephone and call your family as you would like to because it was too expensive.

I began to despise my stepdad even more when he married my mom. He started his role as stepdaddy immediately. He didn't even establish a relationship at first; he immediately started dictating rules and making me and my sister say, "No sir, yes sir; no ma'am and yes ma'am." He was from the south, so that was normal, but not for us northern folks. When he first started telling us to say "yes sir, no sir; no ma'am and yes ma'am," I told him, "I'm not saying that—and you can't make me." Well, my mom stepped in and she enforced it. It felt so awkward because that was not how we were raised.

He started giving me chores to do, which really made me angry. "You are going to start washing your own clothes," he would say.

"Wash my own clothes?? What in the world?! I am way too young to be washing my clothes."

My mom did everything before she married this man. The only thing that I had to do was wash the dishes, and I barely did that. He started teaching me how to sort my clothes. My mom had taught me before, but I still wasn't made to wash my own clothes.

Then he started telling me that I had to clean the bathrooms. To be honest, I didn't mind cleaning the bathrooms; I actually liked it, which is weird. It was the laundry that I didn't like doing.

And of course, my sister and I had to keep our rooms clean—that was a constant struggle. I thought he was the meanest man for making me do chores, but seriously, I am very thankful that he installed responsibility in me in those areas at a young age. I didn't appreciate it until I got older. It's all good now!

The fact that this man—who was not my biological daddy—was telling me what to do, made me feel very angry and bitter towards him. As a matter of fact, my own daddy didn't discipline or rebuke me. I was not used to the rebuke or discipline from a father. That was foreign to my ears.

The absence of discipline from a father plants the seed of rebellion and disobedience. I truly believe there is a difference between the discipline from a father, and the discipline from a mother. When my mom was married to my biological daddy, she did all of the disciplining. My dad never whooped me or yelled at me. The one time he slightly raised his voice at me to get into the car, and it broke me to pieces. I was heartbroken because I wasn't used to any type of discipline from him.

Seeds of Rejection

I would have thought that when my parents divorced, all the household drama was left behind—but it wasn't; it was just another day with a different man. The arguing started between my mother and him. Nothing physical on his part at least, but his words were damaging enough.

I wasn't the best student in elementary. As a matter of fact, I was always getting into trouble, mostly for talking, and the school would call home to my mom. My getting into constant trouble at school did not make my relationship with my stepfather any better. He was always calling me stupid. "You are so stupid." are the words that he uttered on a consistent basis. Hearing the word "stupid" hurt me to my core; it caused me to act out a lot. Not only did he cause deep wounds of hurt—but he watered a seed of rejection. I believe I already had rejection in me while in my mother's womb because of the rejection she experienced while pregnant with me.

Yes, this is possible. From the moment life is breathed in you, the enemy begins a plot against your life. We were born in sin, which tells us that sin can enter in through the mother's womb. The enemy used my stepfather to water the seed of rejection that was already on the inside of me. Did you catch it? The enemy used my stepdad as a vessel to do his work. The rejection I felt from him calling me "stupid" manifested in bitterness towards him, and towards my mother—for marrying him.

I was already angry about being in Germany, and I had a spirit of anger on the inside of me—the devil was able to use him to fuel that anger. I had plenty of angry outbursts, to the point where I would literally destroy my room and go ballistic.

At the time, my mom did not know how to respond to my anger because it appeared more like rebellion, instead of the deep wounds of hurt that they were, which manifested as anger. I had also grown up seeing a lot of anger between my mom and my biological father, and had learnt their behavior because it was modeled to me. On top of those deep layers, there were so many unstable emotions going on in the inside of me. My parents were divorced; my dad abandoned me, a new man came along and then we were shipped to another country. All of this happened in a very short period of time and it can be a lot on any child; I know, it was for me.

My little sister was about four years old when my mom married my stepdad. My sister was very accepting of him and she took to him right away; therefore, he won her over from the start. I, on the other hand, did not give him a chance to win me over. He was not my father, and from the beginning, I gave him a hard time.

Since I was the angry, rebellious, disobedient child—full of hurt and bitterness—I often felt like my little sister was favored over me. In fact, it seems as if she was favored in a sense because she was mild-mannered, and didn't cause trouble. I gave everyone a hard time because of the anger and rejection that I felt inside.

When we went on vacations or family outings, I would purposely distance myself from everyone and I would pout the whole time. I didn't want to be part of the family because I felt like I did not belong. I felt rejected, so I responded with rejection as a defense by distancing myself. I was the one getting in the most trouble, and I was the one that was the most disobedient.

I was so young during this time. In hindsight, I now realize that what I perceived to be favoritism, could have stemmed from the concern that my mom had towards my sister, and the extra care that my sister needed, due to the surgery that she had as a child.

When my sister was a baby, she had major surgery, and I believe my mom took special care and had a closeness to her because of that. For a period of time after the surgery, my sister had to wear a helmet on her head, so that she would not injure herself. The doctor thought she would be slow and would not be able to attend college. However, in high school, my sister was an honor roll student; received a free scholarship to attend a university and graduated with two bachelor's degrees. She has since obtained her Master's degree. The devil said one thing—but God spoke another.

Although I felt my sister was favored; she was still my little sister, and we were very close until I moved out of my mom's house later on in life.

Seeds of Anger and Perversion

As time marched on in Germany, I remained a difficult child. I had an "I don't care" attitude. The seeds of anger from early childhood had germinated into plants. I had frequent anger outbursts and I stayed in trouble at school. I was always on punishment at home.

My punishment was to stay in my room, and I was not allowed to watch T.V. My stepdad would disconnect the T.V. but I would always figure out how to connect it back. I am not sure how I was able to do that, but I guess I was good at figuring things out.

In Germany, on the army base, we did not have cable, so we had a whole lot of VCR movies. Now, along with being disobedient, I was a very curious kid. I would go through the movies, pop one in, and, to my surprise, it would be a nasty pornography movie. Because I was curious and needing entertainment, I would sit and watch it.

One day, I accidently revealed this to my mom. I believe I was asking her questions, and she figured out that I had been watching those movies, so the movies were hidden from me. That took away my entertainment, but the seeds of perversion had already been planted.

I had been watching the movies out of curiosity. I actually thought it was disgusting, but that curiosity opened the door to masturbation. The devil knows that children are curious, and he will use that curiosity to plant seeds. Those seeds will eventually germinate and open up the door to sin. For me, that early exposure to pornography opened the door to masturbation, that lasted for many years. I did not see anything wrong with masturbation, and most people don't, especially those who are single and waiting for their husbands. There was even one point in my life that one of my Christian instructors in college said that God made masturbation for singles. That was all I needed to hear to continue in this sexual sin. Yes, you read it correctly... sexual sin.

Masturbation is excused by some Christians because you are not actually fornicating with a man. However— you are sinning against yourself. You are turning towards yourself to fulfill a need that is only meant for married couples. Not only that, you are fantasizing or creating images in your mind of someone that is not your husband or wife. In a sense, you have created an idol and an act of worship in having an orgasm fulfilled outside of a marriage covenant.

It was only once I had completely surrendered myself to Jesus Christ, that I was able to get free from this spirit.

Seeds of Faith Developing

Although I experienced so many tribulations while in Germany, I also experienced many victories. God had a

purpose in our move to Germany, but where there is purpose; there is also an enemy that is there to kill, steal and
destroy. The devil always has an agenda in everything
that we do; whether good or bad. His agenda is to kill,
steal and destroy whatever he can in your life.

It was in Germany, at the age of nine, that I first accepted Jesus Christ in my life and was baptized. In the United States, we went to church, but we were churchgoers.
You know, the type of church member that just goes on
a Sunday, Wednesday and any other day between, but
has no real personal prayer life, study of God's word or
a solid relationship with God that changes their outward
behavior because of an inward working of the Holy Spirit.

God cared so much about us, that He turned a bad situation around for His purpose; the purpose of knowing
Him in a deeper and more intimate way. It was in Germany that we were first introduced to the power of the Holy
Spirit, and the evidence of speaking in tongues. We lived
on the army base and there was only one church building
which was shared amongst all the denominations.

The first time we went to the church service, I was
amazed at how lively they were. They were clapping
hands, jumping and dancing around; shouting, and
speaking in tongues. I had never been in a church such
as this. I was intrigued and happy to be in such a lively
church with clap-your-hands music, not like the "boring"
church in the States. Back in the States, I had never even
seen a charismatic service, and it was funny how even at
such a young age I desired "more" from the service than
just hymns.

In Germany, it was as if God granted that desire for
"more" of Him without me really knowing what "more"
looked like. I loved going to church—I considered it fun!
My mom got us involved in the church. I was a junior ush-

er and in the children's choir. We had dinner at each other's houses on Sundays and traveled quite a bit to other churches to sing in the choir. It was like we had a new family. We were far away from home, but God gave us a new church family to fulfill the void of family and relationships.

I remember the days when the altar was full and everybody was crying out to God for hours. You would see tears running down people's faces and snot dripping from people's noses. I didn't see anyone running to get Kleenex; it was just raw and vulnerable before God. Some people were tarrying for the Holy Ghost on the altar and nobody was concerned about the time because we were lost in Jesus.

I carried a notebook every time I went to church to write notes during the sermon. I have that same notebook to this day. I wrote down the name of the pastor giving the sermon, the subject of the sermon, the Scriptures, and other important things that he said in his sermon.

The seeds of faith that God planted in my heart during the time we lived with Grammie started to germinate and take root. As I look back on that, I am amazed at the interest that I had in God at such an early age. The life of Jesus Christ became my new norm. I can remember me and my friends playing church; someone was the preacher and we would play as if we were catching the Holy Ghost. I am sure some of you can relate!

It was at this age—nine years old—that I also preached many sermons at home, in front of the mirror. My mom never knew that I did this, but I would be preaching away. I recall making a sermon out of the song "Man in the Mirror" by Michael Jackson... too funny! I wish I could hear some of those sermons that I preached. So when someone asks me how long have I been preaching, my answer is "Since I was nine years old!" I didn't have an audience and I didn't need one.

I never thought that what I was pretending to do at a young age was something that God would use me to do as an adult. I don't remember ever uttering the words *"I want to be a preacher when I grow up."*

But that seed of Jesus was planted in me at a young age, so that one day the seed of His Word would bring great increase in my life. He is the author and the finisher of our faith, and He will complete the work He has begun in us.

"Being confident of this,
that he who began a good work in you will carry it on
to completion until the day of Christ Jesus."
Philippians 1:6

Reconciliation

We stayed in Germany until I was eleven years old. Before we leave that season in my life, I want to tell you how God was faithful to bring about reconciliation between my stepdad and me—years later.

Twenty something years later, I received a phone call from my mom while I was at work. She asked me if I would mind if she gave my stepfather my phone number. I was totally okay with it. He called me and we talked, and it was actually nice to hear from him after all those years. We caught up on what we were doing in life, and he expressed how nice it was to see the woman of God that I had become.

We talked nearly every day for about a month. During one of our conversations, we talked about the hurt that I felt from him calling me "stupid" on so many occasions. He didn't remember his hurtful words and expressed great remorse—he apologized. He said he was young; he had done and said a lot of foolish things during that time that he now regretted. I believe my stepdad had gotten to a place in his life where he needed closure from his past and the things that he has done. It was beautiful that God had brought us together after twenty-something years to talk everything out.

I have forgiven my stepfather and no longer hold any resentment, bitterness or unforgiveness towards him. The Bible says that God makes all things beautiful in His time, and He did just that with this broken relationship.

Chapter 3

A Rebellious Life in Atlanta

When I was about thirteen years old, my mom ended up divorcing my stepdad. She did not want to move back to Battle Creek, Michigan to raise her daughters. I couldn't understand why she didn't want to raise us in Battle Creek, until I became older. I then understood why—there was nothing in Battle Creek for young people to do. And they used to say, "There's nothing in Battle Creek for young people—but trouble." She decided to find a job in Atlanta, and moved us there.

When we arrived in Atlanta, I was a happy kid. I absolutely loved the apartment we were living in. My sister and I shared a bedroom, and my mom had decorated it beautifully. However, I was not one to be cooped up inside. I needed to be out and about during the day. I started hanging out outside and within a short space of time. I had met a lot of friends in the neighborhood.

Believe it or not, the first friends I had were a group of young teenage guys. If I remember correctly, they initially approached me because, obviously, they could tell that I was new in the neighborhood. They were all from different complexes within the same neighborhood and everybody went to different schools. I thought it was cool that although we lived around each other, we didn't all go to the same school. Where I was from, in those days, if you lived in the same neighborhood, you went to the same school.

This group of boys instantly became my homeboys; not one of them became my boyfriend and neither did I like

23

any of them. Don't get me wrong, a few of them were cute, but those were my homeboys.

Since I had a lot of boys as friends, they would call my house all the time. When we moved to Atlanta, my mom reunited with her high school sweetheart, and they ended up getting married. My mom and current stepdad at the time, would get on me constantly because of all the phone calls. They did not like it at all and put a stop to it very quickly. I must admit, I was boy crazy at the time, but most of the boys calling the house were just homeboys. In hindsight, I can see why my parents were upset; I would have felt the same way if I had a daughter!

One of the things that I loved the most about Atlanta was that I met people from all over the United States. There was such a diversity of people and everybody had their own dialect, style and culture. The kids from the North would joke about the kids from the South, and the kids from the South would joke about the kids from the North! The jokes would be about the way we used certain words and our accents, depending on where we were from. It was all in fun and nobody took each other seriously.

Everybody seemed to link up with their own tribe. A group of Michiganders would hang out, and then a group from New York would hang out. I found my tribe; there were four of us in total, but we were not all from the same city or state. One of my friends I met actually lived in a nearby neighborhood. We became best friends.

As time went on, during my ninth-grade year, skipping school became a reality. We were so smooth with it. We would all meet up at my friend's house in the morning and then take turns calling the school, pretending to be each other's mom, to report our absence. Then we would write absence excuse letters and forge our parents' name, to hand into the school office at the end of the day. Despite not attending school in the mornings, we always went back to school at the end of the day and turned in our fake notes to the school's office. Things are so high tech now—you can't get away with truancy the way we did back then!

Now that I think about it, I was very young to be skipping school. I think I was very curious and daring as a teenager to have done these types of things. For example, we would catch the MARTA (Atlanta's transportation) then go downtown Atlanta, and just walk around; how silly. We had no agenda. We were just being rebellious, young teenagers. Another time, one of my friends got a hold of some wine coolers for us to drink. I don't recall getting drunk but I remember having a bit of a buzz.

One day, when we were AWOL, we got into the car with total strangers—a group of teenage boys. Now that was stupid, but that's how we rolled. These guys took us to their parents' house and they were smoking marijuana. I never smoked marijuana during this time and did not want that day to be my first. One of the guys kept coming on to me and it scared me because I was a virgin and had no interest in sex or drugs. Long story short, they ended up dropping us back off because it became a very uncomfortable situation. We never did that again!

I know some of you are probably wondering if my mom ever found out about me skipping school. I believe she had discernment that I was, because one day she started yelling at me saying, "If you are skipping school, you are going to really be in trouble!"

My mom did not play. I did not get the best grades in school, and my mom was the type of mom to put me on punishment until the next report card. I got my grades up because I absolutely could not stand being confined to the house. I liked being outside with my friends. But the punishment did nothing to sort out the rebellion in my heart. With rebellion comes a hard heart, and a heart that is not teachable or trainable.

I know my mom wanted the best for me and probably did not know what to do with me at times. But God had a plan. She happened to find out about a youth service for teenagers only called "Youth for Christ" that was held every Saturday evening.

At the time, I was fourteen years old. I can remember one of the ministers taking me on a walk, and he began to speak words of life into me. I did not know it was called prophecy at the time. He said, "You have the gift of mercy and discernment. You can see things in people that others cannot, and God will use you to pray for others and speak into their lives."

The words he spoke over me got me so excited. I was ready to start working for Jesus. During Youth for Christ, teenagers ran the entire evening service. It was teenagers praying for other teenagers on the prayer line. I admired teenagers praying and speaking life over other teenagers, so when I received that word from the minister, I thought I was going to operate at that present time in my life, just like those teenagers—but that was not so.

I did not start praying or prophesying over other teenagers at the Youth for Christ meetings, but I did start to pray a lot for others during my own prayer time. I started seeing those prayers for others being answered frequently. I enjoyed seeing my prayers answered and loved praying so much that I said there should be a ministry in church where you just pray for others. I had no idea that what I was doing was intercession. I had no idea that a ministry as such ever existed.

God surely met me at a young age and planted many seeds in my heart. During this time in Atlanta, I saw some of the seeds become young plants. But it wasn't long before the devil started to enforce his plot against my life to try and destroy the plan and purpose that God had for my life.

After a while, I no longer felt like I belonged in Atlanta, and started feeling homesick. I wanted to move back to Battle Creek, Michigan with my daddy. My mom was not having it, especially since my dad was a drug addict and was unstable. This was when I found out about his drug habit, but didn't want to believe it. However, despite her fears, I wasn't taking no for an answer and I rebelled even more. I became angry, bitter and frustrated.

My strategy of disobedience and rebellion to get back to Battle Creek finally worked. My mom reached her breaking point and said, "You are moving back to Battle Creek with your dad." However, going back to live with my dad wasn't a reality because of his drug problem. I know he would have taken me in a minute, but his instability prevented him from doing so.

I have a close-knit family so my mom shared what was going on with her sister and one of them volunteered to take me in. I was so homesick that I was fine with that, as long as I could be back in Battle Creek. So, at the age of fifteen, I moved back to Battle Creek.

Chapter 4

Days of My Youth: A Rollercoaster Ride

It Gets Real

I moved in with my aunt and everything was going well. It was just me, my aunt and her husband. My aunt took me to get the things that I needed for the upcoming school year.

Everything was quite laid back at my aunt's house. I did not have too many rules to keep. I didn't even have too many chores. As a matter of fact, I didn't have to wash dishes, which I didn't mind at all. However, I did have some boundaries put on me, which now that I have kids of my own, I understand.

My aunt monitored my whereabouts and wanted to know the life history of all my friends. She wanted to know where they lived, who their parents were, what type of work did their parents do and what kind of car did they drive. I often wondered why all that mattered. Did she need a résumé? It was almost like an interview, and I couldn't just come and go as I pleased.

I felt like a totally different person returning back to Battle Creek; my attitude and mindset were different. I had a hardcore mentality about myself, and even my cousins could see the difference in me. It had been a whole different lifestyle living in Atlanta. Every city has its own culture, and when you are in an environment for so long, you begin to take on its traits. Atlanta wasn't about being soft, or a pushover. You had to be tough, at least, that's how I felt and what I experienced during my time there.

Once I started school, I tried hanging around my old elementary friends. I hung out with them for a while, but then it started to feel awkward. Slowly but surely, I stopped hanging around my old group. I no longer felt like I fitted in with them. I had been gone from Battle Creek since my fourth-grade year in elementary, and I had returned in my sophomore year. During the time away, I had seen a lot—good and bad; and experienced a lot—good and bad. I had changed.

My desire had always been to graduate from Battle Creek Central High School because all my older cousins had graduated from there. I had also suffered plenty of whoopings and punishments to get back to Battle Creek. So, despite not feeling like I fitted in, I stayed at the high school, but left my old friendships.

Battle Creek was way behind Atlanta in fashion, slang and music, so naturally, I felt out of place and different. I had a different style in clothes and even my slang was different so much so that I had to teach one of my cousins the meaning behind my slang. I was the "slang queen" at the time, which my mom hated. She would always tell me to speak English. "Anyways", at the time, I wore these boots that nobody in my school was wearing. We called them Jodeci boots—after a R&B group. I brought a lot of attention to my boots and the next thing I knew, everybody was starting to get the Jodeci boots, but I was already ahead of the game. One of the girls at school befriended me, then asked to wear my boots, and I let her. Why I did that I don't know, because she messed up my boots! Never again! However, despite the boot incident, this girl became my new friend and hanging out partner.

It was during this time that I was influenced to start smoking marijuana. One day, we went off the school grounds for lunch and my new friend pulled out a joint and asked me if I wanted to try it. I was game. I knew what marijuana was, but had just never tried it before. I tried it, and actually liked it. After that, every day we would leave for lunch to go smoke, and I would return back to school as high as a kite, eyes low—with the giggles. But by the grace of God, and His hand on my life despite me being lost, I didn't become an addict or what we called in my day, a "weed head." I didn't have to have it day in and day out.

In those days, smoking weed as a sophomore in high school was nothing new or uncommon. Back then, classmates would walk down the halls yelling, "I got two blunts for sell: two for $10 or one for $5." It was pretty normal to hear stuff like that through the halls. I started hanging out and meeting new people; smoking and drinking on the weekends became my thing to do.

One of my new friends became my best friend and she had a driver's license. Her parents would let her use the car on the weekends. I was always trying to be at her house during weekends because she had a level of freedom that I did not have. Plus, her mom was so cool with a big heart. She treated me like her own. I was a part of the family. It was a given that I was going to be there on the weekends.

Hanging out in the streets, joy riding and hooking up with friends was our thing. We already smoked weed, but wanted to step it up a notch, and drink some liquor. Some of the guys that we started hanging out with were already into drinking liquor, but drinking was new to us. One night we were all hanging out, and I got drunk for the first time, at the age of fifteen.

That night, I was staying over at my friend's house. We went to hang out at her sister's house and decided there that we wanted to get drunk. I do not remember what I was drinking at the time, but I was totally out of it. I had to be carried into the bedroom to lie down, and I do remember feeling so horrible, but I couldn't express how horrible I felt because I literally could not talk as I was so messed up. My curiosity about getting drunk was fulfilled, but now I wanted to see what all the talk was about sex.

At school, in class, I often heard my friends talk about sex, and when they would talk, I could not respond at all because I was a virgin. I got tired of being excluded from the conversations—peer pressure got me! I decided I was going to have sex.

One Friday afternoon, afterschool, I said, "This weekend I am going to have sex"; I committed a willful sin of fornication. There was a guy that I was already hanging out with on the weekends, and I liked him, but we were not having sex. I decided that I was going to have sex with him that weekend. I told him that I was ready to lose my virginity. I was totally scared, but I was tired of feeling like I was the only virgin on the planet. I didn't have enough self-worth and remember, while growing up, I was not validated by my father; therefore, I did not see any value in being a virgin. My value and self-worth were based on how well I was accepted by others; how well I fitted in. I finally calmed my nerves down enough to have sex. I lost my virginity at the young ripe age of fifteen years old, which is way too young to be having sex, but as I stated before, the younger the enemy can get you, the better. When you are young, you are vulnerable and easily persuaded.

You would think that since my curiosity was fulfilled, I would be through with sex, especially since it wasn't all that I imagined it would be. Nope. Remember the early exposure to porn in Germany? The enemy was watering the seed of perversion that was already on the inside of me from a child. That seed started to germinate and grow.

By this time, I was living with my mom again in Battle Creek. I started liking this other guy at school a lot. He would ask me to come over to his house after school. When I was living with my mom, I had to ask permission before I did anything. I mustered up enough nerve to ask her if I could go over to this boy's house. I already knew the answer, but I wanted to ask anyway. My mom kept telling me, "You already know what he wants from you. No, you can't go over there."

Well, yeah, I knew what he wanted. But I also wanted it because, as I said, there was an attraction there. I was no longer a virgin; therefore, I was already open to sexual sin. He used protection, but the condom broke. It still did not cross my mind that I was going to end up pregnant. Well, I did end up pregnant. My grandmother used to tell me that all it takes is one time—she was right. I wasn't a virgin, but it was our first time, and that is all it took.

I was so terrified to tell my mom I was pregnant. I did not know how I was going to tell her, so I decided to write her a letter and put it on her bed. I did not have enough guts to tell her face-to-face. When I came home from school, the letter was still on her bed, but, as soon as she arrived home from work, I knew that she had read it. I could see her angry expression as she climbed out of the car. She slammed the door and walked very quickly into the house. She was livid!

She did not want me to have the baby. I was only sixteen and I was eight weeks pregnant. Back then, my mom was not where she is today in her spiritual walk so she suggested that I have an abortion. She was concerned that I wouldn't finish high school. I assured her that I was going to finish high school; an abortion was not an option for me. I told God, "Let your Will be done." I was not going to have an abortion. I put it all in God's hands. Needless-to-say, I had a miscarriage and I experienced actual labor during this miscarriage.

It was heartbreaking for me to miscarry because I had begun to prepare myself to have a baby. I wanted the baby—in truth, I wanted a baby to fill the void from the rejection and abandonment that I felt. I wanted a baby to love. I often thought, *"I am going to show my baby the love that I wanted to experience."* I thought that having a baby was going to make everything alright.

Chapter 5

How Freedom Lured Me

After my miscarriage, I started having ambitions to attend college after high school. I was wanting the independence and freedom that I craved.

I felt as if Battle Creek was not good for me, and that there was too much negativity around me. I had wanted to come back to Battle Creek so badly, but after I returned and time went on, I regretted my decision. I couldn't see any opportunities for young people. Furthermore, I was making wrong decision after wrong decision because of that environment.

I have often played back in my mind how life would have been if I hadn't come back to Battle Creek. I didn't feel like Battle Creek was where I was supposed to be. Well, the Bible states that God works everything out for the good for those that are called according to His purpose. And looking back, I can see how God did indeed work all things out for the good. However, at that time, I didn't see me being called for a purpose at all in Battle Creek. College was the one way that I was going to leave Battle Creek—and get back on track.

Initially, my mom didn't want me to go away to college. Her concern was that she wanted to make sure college was for me and it was something that I really wanted to do. Well, it was something I really wanted to do. My school age friend and I always talked about attending college and sharing dorms together. I talked about going away to college all through high school.

As part of my plans to get to college, I was accepted into a summer program called Upward Bound. Upward Bound is a program that prepares you for college. I even had a chance to stay on a college campus during the summer; now that was no joke!

The dorms were crazy hot. We had to wake up at 5:00 a.m. every morning and we walked to every class with heavy backpacks on our backs. Some of our classes were way across campus. We couldn't wait to go home for the weekends. However, despite this experience, it still didn't take away my desire to attend college because in my mind, I was going to be moving away to college. I always wanted to go away and move out of Battle Creek.

But my ambitions and reality were two different things. I ended up not being able to leave Battle Creek to attend college, so I decided to attend the local community college—Kellogg Community College. I was planning to start the summer after graduation.

When I knew that I wasn't going away to college after high school, I began to crave freedom in another way, and I set my mind on getting my own apartment. I was determined to get it, no matter what. I was rebellious, which meant that I was disobedient and did not like to follow rules or authority. Lakeea wanted to do what Lakeea wanted to do! I did not like limitations put on me. I wanted to get out on my own as fast as I could.

So, during twelfth grade, I began to plan. I got a job at McDonald's and started earning an income. During that year, I bought things to prepare for my own apartment. I bought myself a set of dishes and even a trashcan for the bathroom. I was so determined.

My best friend at the time fell pregnant in high school, and ended up getting her own place while we were still in high school. Having a baby gave her an advantage to have her own apartment, and the ability to receive assistance from the state. She knew all of the ropes pertaining to getting help, and I learned a lot from her; she was a good resource for me.

After graduation, at the age of seventeen, I started looking for an apartment. She referred me to the landlord who had given her one. This lady showed me a bedroom that I could rent in one of her houses, and then showed me an efficiency apartment in another one of her houses. Of course, I opted for the efficiency apartment because I would be on my own.

When I first moved into my apartment, it felt quite weird to be on my own. I didn't have to ask if I could go this place or that place. I didn't have a curfew. Wow, I was free to answer to only me. It felt pretty good!!

My apartment was very small, with a tiny kitchen and stove with hardly any room to cook. The bathroom was so small that you could not actually lie down in the bathtub if you wanted to; even the toilet seat was tiny. I didn't know that they made bathtubs and toilet seats that small, but it didn't matter because I was independent.

I went out and bought a showerhead to fix the small bathtub problem, but the people that lived below me complained that the water was dripping down to their apartment. Huh?!? Well, my first thought was that the landlord should fix it. But nope, she was not willing to fix it, and told me to take down the showerhead. I couldn't put up a fight because she was renting the apartment out illegally—yes, she was a slumlord, and besides this, she knew that I was a young teenager that did not want to go back home to my aunt or mother.

The leaking bath wasn't the only issue with the apartment; it didn't have a phone jack or cable cords. Before I moved in, I had specifically asked her if those things were available, and of course she said yes. She was all about the money. I had to use the payphone down the street if I needed to use a phone; there weren't cell phones in those days. But it didn't matter to me if I had to walk to the pay-phone at one or two in the morning—I had no fear.

To add to these minor issues, I also started to experience a horrible smell that lingered in the hall of the entire apartment house. The smell would find its way into my apartment. My neighbor right across the hall was on drugs and he was the culprit! There was a large gap underneath my door and I used to put a towel across the gap to try to block the smell. The gap was so big that a small creature could easily fit underneath it, and guess what... I did have some unwelcome house guests!

First the mice started appearing. I couldn't stand mice. I could remember mice getting into my grandmother's house, and I would literally jump on top of the table screaming if I saw one. Then the cockroaches appeared. I was very uncomfortable with the fact that I was now living with roaches, but it didn't make me uncomfortable enough to move. We were just going to be one big happy family. All of this just for freedom.

Fortunately, I didn't spend a whole lot of time there because I worked in the evenings, and as soon as I got off work, it was time to hang out with my friends. My best friend lived right across the street from me, and we spent most of our evenings playing cards, drinking and getting high. Nobody had cable so there wasn't anything else to do. As a matter of fact, that was "life" to me because my vision was clouded. All I knew was, I was on my own; and I could hang out as long as I wanted to, and I could go where I wanted to.

The Cost of Freedom

At this point in my life, I still had ambitions to attend Kellogg Community College (KCC) in the summer and I wanted to use my own income, without financial aid, because I was not living with my mom.

When I enquired at the college, I was told that in order for them to use my income only, I would have to be twenty-six years old. My heart sank. "Really! Twenty-six years old?" Then the receptionist said, "Or if you have kids, then you could use your own income." I became very discouraged at that moment. I was thinking, "What type of mess is this? I must have kids to get help... so not cool."

I decided to go down to the welfare office to see if I could qualify for anything. I knew I should qualify for food stamps, and a Medicaid card. The intake worker at the welfare office asked me a series of questions. She discovered that I qualified to get a welfare check at the age of seventeen years old because I fell under some program for "youth taking care of themselves". I can't remember the exact type of program and I'm not sure if this program still exists. I was working at McDonald's and receiving food stamps, a Medicaid card and a welfare check, with no kids —at seventeen years old.

I finally enrolled in college; however, it didn't take long for me to drop out. The sun would be shining brightly while I was sitting in class, and all I could think about was hanging out with my friends. In college, there is no pressure for you to succeed; no pressure to complete your homework or be on time for class. If I wanted to walk out of class to hang out, that is what I could do, without having to worry about getting on punishment. You are completely responsible for your own decisions. My priorities were all messed up. I dropped out of college to hang out and run the streets with my homies.

Freedom suited me, so I started to hang out a little more. My best friend and I started hanging out with a couple of our homeboys. We were a crew that was together every night, joy riding, smoking marijuana, and drinking on a regular basis.

There were times that we were so messed up that we ended up in another city. During a good night, we got hotel rooms. Someone looking from the outside in, would have thought we were getting hotel rooms to have sex ... Nope that wasn't the case. We needed a spot to chill because by this time I moved back in with my aunt, my homeboys stayed with their parents, and my friend was not in her own place. We wanted our privacy to get our buzz on; it wasn't the best thing to be riding around drinking and smoking.

When I turned eighteen, I entered into freedom on a whole other level. In my eyes, I thought I was now old enough to go clubbing—though in the eyes of the law, it was illegal.

At the time my aunt owned a club, so I felt as if I had clout. I was standing in the line ready to go in the club. I handed over my I.D., and the guy said, "You are not twenty-one." I wasn't hearing it! I told him to let me in because my aunt owned the club and next thing I knew, I was in. The first person I saw was my uncle, and the first thing he said was, "What are you doing in here?" I told him, "It's my birthday," as if that justified me being illegally in the club.

I wasn't a regular at the clubs because I did not want to be that person with the reputation of being a "regular". Battle Creek was a small town, and everybody knew everybody, so I wanted to keep a low profile. I was starting not to "fit in" anyway again. At least, that's what I was being told.

Chapter 6

Listening to God's Voice

"Suppose one of you has a hundred sheep and loses
one of them. Doesn't he leave the ninety-nine in the
open country and go after the lost sheep
until he finds it?" Luke 15:4

I thank God for chasing me in the middle of my mess.
He was preparing me for repentance, while I was yet in
the world. Even while I was in the world, God was showing me that He had called me and set me apart. He was
showing me that the life that I was living was not for me;
I did not fit in even when I was partaking in sin.

As I mentioned previously, I was not a regular clubgoer,
but I would occasionally go. There was one time that I
went to the club and this guy, from California, approached
me and said, "I've never seen you before, you don't even
look like you belong in here, you're not even dressed like
you belong in here; you are a businesswoman." *What did
he just say?? He betta prophesy!*

He was speaking prophetically into my life and didn't
even know it. Before I continue, let me explain. I was not
in the club with a blazer and dress pants on or dressed
like a businesswoman. I actually had on some fitted jeans,
these bad pumps, and a hot shirt; but I guess he saw a
business woman in the club that did not fit in.

"You don't dress like you belong here." The other young
man that stated similar words was referring to me not
dressing like I was from Battle Creek; we were actually

going to junior college at the time and having a conversation after class. The second similar comment wasn't from a club scene this particular time.

Those words would totally puzzle me at the time, because I wasn't dressed in designer clothes, but they saw something. I guess I carried myself in a way that I didn't realize; I carried myself in a way that let the world know and say, "You don't belong on this side of the fence," but I was trying to belong; I was trying to fit in.

I believe God was using those moments to let me know that I was set apart, and even those in the world recognized that I was set apart. I remember another guy telling me, "You are the business one out of the crew—you are different." Looking back, I can see that God was speaking business in my ears for a long time.

I yearned for the affection from a man, and I was hearing things like, "You don't belong here; you are about your business; you are different." These words were from guys that were the total opposite of what God wanted for my life.

I guess God was speaking to me then, saying, *"You are fearfully and wonderfully made—set apart for a purpose."* But I could not hear Him speak because of all the confusion in my heart.

I was drawn to guys that had some class but street in them. I mostly ended up with drug dealers. There were some moments that it was what it was—a physical thing, an attraction; and then there were other moments when I really started feeling for the guy and hoped it would last forever. There was one drug dealer that I fell in love with; at times, I would be right there with him at the drug spots.

I should have recognized early on that God had set me apart because while I was at those drug spots, I would be trying to talk sense into people that were doing destructive things—like getting drunk and even having sex outside of marriage.

There were times, when I was high on marijuana, and I would start to talk about deep and spiritual things. In the middle of smoking weed, I would bust out with a sermon. Who does that? Me! It was very common for me to start speaking on the things of God when I was in a high or drunken state. I had a friend that did similar things when we went out to the clubs. It was as if we were the best witnesses in our sin and all. I would see someone totally drunk, and I would be the one saying, "You know you shouldn't be getting drunk like that!" My friends would actually listen to me; they would say things like "Lakeea gets real deep when she is high, but it be good."

I had expectations of myself in my own way, although my expectations were not high enough for me to remain a virgin until marriage. It is funny, my main message while living in sin, was on fornication—God was speaking to me heavily to stop fornicating. I was preaching against the very things that I was partaking in. I remember talking about how wrong fornication was and how you become one with the person that you are having sex with. There was one time I even took a video of a sermon over to my friend's house. As a matter of fact, it was Juanita Bynum's sermon on "No More Sheets." Boy, did my homeboy get offended by that sermon! The Holy Spirit was convicting.

The teachings of Jesus were hidden in my heart, but I was under the bondage of the enemy. I was not a very good representation of Jesus Christ by the way I was living, but the Word of God never ceased from coming out of me despite my sin. I was even told by one of my friends during that time that I was a "cool" Christian. I knew I wasn't a cool Christian, and that the things that I was doing were wrong, but I wasn't ready to surrender to the Lord completely.

I was still seeking validation and love to fill that empty void. I had sought it from men, but now I longed for a baby. I thought that a baby would fill those areas of rejection and abandonment. I was in a relationship with my high school sweetheart at the time, and he expressed to me one day that he wanted a baby. That was music to my ears; I instantly stopped taking my birth control shots, and it didn't take long for me to fall pregnant at the young ripe age of eighteen years old. I wanted a boy—and I was given a boy. My life slowly began to shift in the right direction, because now I had someone else to care for. However, I still had that empty void which I continued to try to fill...

After our son was born, things began to change in my relationship with my high school sweetheart, and we went our separate ways. I found another man that I was attracted to. It was not a relationship—it was an attraction, and I fell pregnant. There was no way that I could have another baby... no way! We weren't in a serious relationship, and two children with two different fathers, was not what I imagined for myself. I thought of myself as better than that, but what did I expect? I wasn't on birth control, or the best birth control there is, which is abstinence. I had an abortion!

However, three months later, I was pregnant again. How foolish, but I was blinded and living for the devil. I contemplated getting another abortion, but I couldn't. I just couldn't do it a second time! Abortions were not going to be my means of birth control. God brought me through and used these precious children to draw me closer to Him and onto His path for my life.

Years later, when I completely surrendered to God, I asked Him why I did all those things and He said, "Because of that which was in your heart."

I had sought validation and affirmation from guys because I didn't have it from my father. I thought that relationships and sexual intimacy would fill the yearning for love and acceptance—those empty spaces in my heart. I was looking to the world to fulfill those voids. I was trying to fulfill them through smoking weed, drinking and young men. I didn't realize that it was the love of Jesus that I needed and yearned for. However, all those bad decisions that did not line up with the Word of God did come with consequences. Sin breeds consequences.

Jesus forgives us of our sin when we go to Him with a sincere heart and ask forgiveness, but that does not stop the consequences of sin. He can withhold the penalty that we so deserve and have mercy upon us, but that sin can leave demonic spirits and strong holds in our souls when they are not dealt with. My life had begun to shift towards Jesus, but my journey of deliverance from bondage to freedom and wholeness, had only just begun.

Chapter 7

Motherhood and the World of Endless Possibilities

*For the Lord watches over the way of the righteous,
but the way of the wicked leads to destruction.
Psalm 1:6*

I now had two children by the age of twenty-one and my eyes began to open even wider. My thinking was starting to change and my life started to take a drastic shift towards the better. I no longer thought just about "me." I had two lives to care for. Two lives that were depending on me, and every decision that I made, whether it was good or bad, would ultimately affect them. I wanted what was best for them. I was willing to do whatever I could, within reason, to make sure they were alright.

My sons are two years and nine months apart to be exact. I had a diaper bag in one hand, a baby in the other, and a little toddler—all at the same time. For the mothers out there with little children, you know what I am talking about, especially when you have one baby car seat and one booster seat; getting two babies together and strapped in the car is no joke—but I managed! I was and still am blessed to have a mothering, nurturing spirit about myself.

It didn't take long for me to adjust to having two little ones. It was a natural progression from having one little one. But I was a little wiser with my youngest son. I didn't go crazy buying brand name clothing or toys that he was too little to play with, or even think about.

When my oldest son was the only child, I went all out and bought him brand name clothes, shoes, and a closet full of toys and teddy bears. I even bought him a ride-on car that he did not think about riding until he was three years old.

My mom kept telling me to stop buying him brand name everything and going all out because he would expect it and I was spoiling him, but he was my only child; plus, I was a teenager and young myself.

This was when I first messed up my credit. I was buying my son all types of clothes. I applied for all of the department store credit cards, and once I got approved, I would run them up to the max. I had no idea about credit scores and spending only 30% of your credit limit. I wasn't very good at paying my credit card bills on time either. At the time, I had no sense of responsibility in this area.

A side note to all parents: teach your children the importance of good credit, budgeting and saving money while they are young. I will cover more information on maintaining a good credit report and other helpful tips in the second half of this book.

I was excellent at caring for the needs of my children—but went overboard in my spending. I wanted to always make sure they were okay; they had become my number one priority.

Careers

Before I had my first child, I was working in a factory. I was hired not too long after I graduated from high school and was making good money. Once I had my firstborn, it was no longer just getting myself ready for work: I had to shift my whole life, and it was a big adjustment. I ended up being at least a minute late for work nearly every day, until I was pointed out. I was fired! I thought that day was the worst day of my life, but in all actuality, it was the best day of my life.

Initially I was discouraged, but my mom encouraged me and told me not to get depressed, that everything was going to be alright. I believed her; and I was very resilient. I didn't stay discouraged for long. I was one to use whatever resources available to me that would help me to have a better life for myself and my son.

Since in the past, I had received assistance without children, so I knew I could get some help with children. I went down to the welfare office to apply for assistance. At the time, the only thing that I qualified for was childcare assistance and Medicaid. However, because I had lost my job, I was able to get food stamps. I was excited about that. How many of you know that when you have food stamps, you buy topnotch expensive steak; you will use your own money to pay for food that you normally wouldn't buy.

My caseworker sent me on a job skills preparation course for about a week. I was required to attend this course if I was to be considered for cash assistance. However, in order to get cash assistance, you had to be making next to nothing. I knew that was not going to work for me because the assistance was not enough to pay my bills or take care of my children, let alone all the other expenses such as rent, a car note and groceries.

During the course, they informed us that they would pay for your interview clothes and your first week of work clothes. They would even pay for a nursing assistant certificate. This was music to my ears. I hated working in the factory and this was my opportunity to get out. I expressed my interest in getting my nursing assistant certificate. I saw an opportunity—and went after it.

I was so determined to succeed that I would stay after class and talk to some of the workers. I wanted whatever help and knowledge that would assist me in finding a new job that was not in a factory. One of the ladies told me about a lady that she knew, that had her own assisted living business. This business owner, was also once on a welfare. She connected me to this lady for a job.

I showed initiative and determination to be better. I wasn't using the system as my lifetime goals or plans: I used the system as a stepping stone, and a way to network other possibilities that may have been available to me.

As I already stated, I was resilient and did not have time to wait until I finished obtaining my nursing assistant license—I had mouths to feed. So, I started working another factory job temporarily through the temp agency. Once I had finished the nursing assistant training, I immediately started job hunting in that field.

At the time, there were temp agencies for nursing assistants that paid well. I managed to get forty hours a week. This lasted for a while, but I eventually found a permanent job at one of the nursing homes. Being a nursing assistant paid the bills and got me out of the factory, but that too was getting old and stale; I still had a yearning and desire for something different.

I am one that loves the new. I get bored if I am doing the same old thing for too long. My wiring is "what's next." Being put in a box and confined to the same old thing for too long makes me miserable and uninterested. This is how God has wired me in every aspect; I do not like routine. Routine is okay for a period of time, but then the routine has to be shaken up a bit. Don't misunderstand me, my not liking routine for so long doesn't mean that I am not disciplined. I am disciplined to pray and read my

Word daily, but it may not be the same time every day. I am disciplined to fast, but it may not be the same type of fast every time. I am disciplined in attending church, but I do not like a set-in-stone program every Sunday. I enjoy putting on diversity events at my job, but I don't have the same speaker every year... you get the picture.

I loved caring for the elderly, but it was time for something new; it was time for an advancement. My sons awakened my desire for more—they gave me a sense of purpose beyond myself. It was no longer about hanging out or wasting my days without a plan to succeed. They were, and still are, my reason; my purpose.

At the center of my heart, God has now put my husband and my children, but back then, before marriage, He used my children to keep me pressing forward. When I had them, an unbreakable bond formed, and I truly believe God put them at the center of my heart to keep me focused, because it was not all about me. Giving up or not reaching higher, was NOT an option. My "yes" then, and my "yes" now, depends on their purpose and destiny in God.

I really did not know what I was going to do next, but I knew that I did not want to be a nursing assistant any longer. One day, I was at home watching T.V. and a commercial came on advertising this technical school that offered training for medical assistants, licensed practical nurses, phlebotomists (medical professionals trained to draw blood for blood tests), or massage therapists. I was intrigued and wanted more information. I was interested in the medical assistant certificate. It appeared to be an easier route than the licensed practical nurse (LPN), although I was going to be learning a lot of the same things. The medical assistant course was not as long as the LPN course, and I was determined to move on from being a nursing assistant—as soon as possible.

Once I have set my mind to do something, I am not one that likes to procrastinate. The training required me to have clinical internship hours. I trained in an orthopedic office for a minimal amount of time and then I began to talk to the Lord. I wanted a full-time internship that would allow me to get my hours done quickly—and get paid. This was a desire of mine that fell right into my lap. I was skimming through the Want Ads in the newspaper and came across a medical assistant job. I called and had an interview; it was the same doctor's office that delivered my two sons. I was already set up for favor!

During the interview, I explained that I needed intern hours in order to receive my medical assistant certificate. The doctor said, "Can you use this job as your intern hours?" What did this man just say?! "Yes, of course," I stated. It was a prayer answered. God opened the door right up for me! To God be the Glory!

I was pleased to be in a new job, in a new environment. I learned how to adapt to the different personalities of the doctors, and their individual expectations. The standard was very high. You hardly got away with making a mistake; you had better not make the same mistake twice! It was crucial to get things right because we were dealing with people, and mistakes could be very serious. I learned fairly quickly. I worked at the doctor's office for a while, and, as I stated earlier about staying in the same old place for too long, I started wanting to move on to something new.

I started having the desire to join the military. I was at work reading the Want Ads, and found an ad regarding joining the reserves. This was going to be "Plan A." At the time, my boys were little, and I already had the plan that my mom could keep them while I went through boot camp. I called my mom up, while I was at work, and told her that I wanted to join the military; she said, "Who's keeping the boys?" And you know my response, "You." And you can guess her response, "I don't think so!" So much for plan A...

I absolutely love the military; I love what they stand for, the discipline, the no-excuse clause and the comradery between each other. I never got to join the military then, but I married a Marine—Semper Fi (the USA Marine's motto meaning "always faithful" or "always loyal"); therefore, I am an honorary Veteran. The Lord still granted my desire in His own unique way. Since the military was not an option, it was time to think of Plan B.

Plan B

> All things are possible to him who believes.
> Mark 9:23

It was time for me to go back to college, and this time I wanted to finish my studies—and finish them quickly. "Let's get it, and quickly" was my motto. I decided to sign up for junior college and enroll in the Human Services program.

At the time, I was living in a housing where the rent was determined by my income. I decided that I was going to work part-time, and attend school full-time. God took care of my children and myself for an entire year. I made only $12,000 that year: God supernaturally took care of us! It still amazes me how we made it through.

When God has His hand on something, He always works it out and makes a way. God always blesses what He puts His hands on. It is so worth being in God's will because He opens doors and releases His favor upon you to accomplish every purpose in your life.

During my time at the junior college, I learned about adult education. I could go to class once a week in the evening and in two years, I will have my bachelor's degree. This was music to my ears! I started working full-time, went to junior college, and the university—all at the same time, in order to get my bachelor's degree. I continued going to junior college because there were classes that I could transfer over to the university. I was determined to make a better life for my children and myself. They were my motivation. One of my cousins looked after the children for me and my time with them was very limited. But I kept telling myself, *"It's just temporary, it will be over soon."*

When I obtained my bachelor's degree in Family Life Education, I decided that I would never be away from my boys for that long again. That sacrifice was complete, and I was not willing to make another one like that while they were little. I took a small break from studying once I graduated, but I still felt as if my goal was incomplete. I had an instructor in junior college that consistently encouraged me and spoke life into me. She stated that I was to be a doctor (Ph.D.), and my minimal was a Master's degree. Her words never left me; she planted a seed in me because she believed in me. I enrolled in the Master's program in Counseling Psychology. I always had aspirations to be a Psychologist since I was a young girl. I had declared it over my life a lot growing up—and it never left.

Grad school was going well, and I met some new friends. I was passing all of my classes, and I looked forward to having my own business as a psychologist one day. However, that was all to change...

During that time, I began to get closer to God and learn more about Him. One of my classes talked a lot about philosophy; things that I was in total disagreement with. I could not get my mind off the Lord, and the things of God. I tried to concentrate in class, but couldn't. I was in disagreement with everything that was being taught, and

I remember sitting in class thinking, *"How am I going to start out working in an organization, under the principles of these beliefs, without me saying something about mine?"* I kept thinking, *"I will get fired!"*

This internal disagreement caused my interest in completing the Master's program in Counseling Psychology to go. Besides losing interest, I could no longer see myself talking to clients all day, everyday for one-hour sessions. Although, I never completed my Master's degree... guess what? I now use the skill set practically every day. It was not a waste.

God has given me a natural ability to counsel, empower, uproot, tear down and rebuild. I love to work with individuals that are ready to go to the next level; people that are ready to grow and be challenged. I absolutely love it!!

Career Challenges

> I can do all things through Christ
> which strengtheneth me.
> Phil 4:13 (*KJV*)

I remember taking on a new job as an Equal Employment Opportunity Manager (EEO). I was not qualified to be an EEO Manager, but I was going through on-the-job training that was supposed to last for two years. This was a paid intern assignment. Within six months of my training, my supervisor was promoted and transferred to a new job. When he left for his promotion, I was offered the position as manager. Here I was supposed to receive two years training, and I only received six months. I had learned quite a bit in those six months, but not everything. I had often hidden behind my supervisor, and avoided speaking with leadership one-on-one, because I was not confident in my ability. However, despite this lack of confidence, I accepted the job.

I went out and bought a plaque to put in my office that stated: *I can do all things through Christ that gives me strength.* I needed to constantly remind myself, *"With Christ, I can accomplish every difficult task on this job."* I could no longer hide behind my supervisor, because he wasn't there; I didn't have a choice but to step out of my comfort zone in faith.

Before I started the job, I had preparation sessions to give me a foundation and a good start. However, I had to continue to read and connect with other EEO managers that were experts in the profession. It was my responsibility to become proficient in the job and God gave me the needed wisdom and knowledge because I kept Him at the center.

However, despite this, there were times that I would get frustrated and stressed because of learning new things. I had to train the staff on my limited knowledge, and I was extremely fearful of speaking in front of employees. I often looked at how big the task or project was, and sized it up before I even began. Based on how challenging the project looked, I would begin to complain, murmur and talk in defeat. Sometimes my words were, *"I can't do this, but I will try."* I was willing to try so that it wouldn't be as if I hadn't even tried, but in the back of my mind I was thinking, *"There is no way that I will be able to do this."* I had already determined in my mind that I was going to fail before I had started. Not realizing that it was never in my ability in the first place. God put me in that position so that I would depend on Him and had to seek Him, not looking at what "I" was not able to accomplish. I learned that through Him, I could do all things—and you can do all things through Him too.

God will never call you to a purpose that you are able to accomplish on your own because you are His ambassador; His workmanship for His Glory! As I look back, I can see the growth that occurred and the boldness that I developed through those challenges. Before long, I gained influence and respect in my position, and walked in it with confidence and courage. When new tasks came about, I was equipped to take them head-on without fear.

Chapter 8

TransHERmation: Giving Birth to the Fruit of the Spirit

As I mentioned a while back, I truly believe God starts to prepare you for repentance while you are still a sinner in the world. He chases you until you finally get tired and say, "Yes...I surrender." God had steadily chased me throughout my life. He had planted seeds and watered them. He had spoken to me through believers and non-believers. He had even spoken to me through my own sermons—remember when I used to preach to the lost while still in my sin?

Psalm 91:11-12 says, "For he will command his angels concerning you to guard you in all your ways; they will lift you up in their hands, so that you will not strike your foot against a stone." God commanded Psalm 91 over my life when I was living in the world. He created me and knows me better than I know myself. He could see in the inner depths of my heart, and see an image of Him planted in me. He continued to water that seed throughout my life—until I reached my breaking point.

I was almost thirty and I can remember it as if it was yesterday. I was sitting on my couch at home, and I was talking to Jesus. I began to share with Him how I was tired of running; tired of having one foot in and one foot out. I told Jesus I was ready to surrender to His Will, and wanted my destiny to be fulfilled; I wanted everything He had for me. So, I finally surrendered and said, *"Yes."*

It was in this moment that I began to pray and read the Bible more. My bed was covered with at least two Bibles, and other Christian books that I was reading. I was hungry and thirsty, and wide open to receive everything that God had for me. I was open to learn and get to know Him in an intimate way. I would spend hours reading the Word, and when I say "hours," I mean *hours*. It got to the point where the Holy Spirt said, "You have other things to do, you cannot just read all day." I was getting addicted to reading the Bible y'all!

My journey of God bringing forth the increase in my life had started. The increase manifested by Him removing the filth and residue of sin from my life. It began the journey of our friendship. I remember God telling me, "Your life has now begun."

In other words, I did not have life until I met Him. The Bible says in Ephesians 2:1-2, "As for you, you were dead in your transgressions and sins, in which you used to live when you followed the ways of this world and of the ruler of the kingdom of the air, the spirit who is now at work in those who are disobedient." The devil will deceive you and make you think that you are "living" when you are hanging out with friends partying, drinking, smoking and having sex. Maybe you didn't, or are not doing those things, but you have not surrendered your life totally to Christ. It doesn't matter what lifestyle you are living, if it is not a lifestyle in Jesus Christ, then you are not living.

I surrendered to Jesus, and the cost of trading my old lifestyle for His, was worth the sacrifice. He would wake me up in the wee hours of the morning to talk to me. He would teach me things that I never knew; the unfolding of the revelations from His Word inspired me to keep pursuing Him as He pursued me. It was amazing to experience Him like I did; it was not burdensome. I was hungry for Jesus and wanted everything He had for me.

A short while after I had said yes to God, I remember going to the Christian bookstore and asking God, "What book should I get?" He led me to a book entitled *Rules of Engagement* by Dr. Cindy Trimm. It is a book on spiritual warfare and warfare prayers. I read that book and the spiritual warfare prayers faithfully. I never knew about spiritual warfare, and had never heard the terminology that she was using in the prayers. Little did I know that He was getting ready to prepare me for battle. Little did I know that He was getting ready to develop a warrior in me.

My life took a drastic shift while reading that book. I can remember reading a part in the book that said something like the only way to learn how to fight, is to be put in a battle. I did not know that after reading those prayers, I would literally be put in a battle to engage with the enemy. I experienced the worst attack of my life, and guess where the enemy hit—my mind.

The Battlefield

Remember at the beginning of this book I told you about the battlefield in my mind, where it felt as if I had several guns pointing at me? Well this was that battle, and it was a tough one.

The accuser of the brethren, the devil, first started tormenting me with my past and the memories of being a fornicator. Day and night, I cried out to God on my knees—asking for forgiveness. I was being tortured with condemnation. I could not grasp that once I ask for forgiveness and turn from my evil ways, I am forgiven. I could not understand that He could wash me whiter than snow. My sin was ever before me. I thought He was so angry with me and that I was somehow being punished endlessly for my past mistakes. I continued to read the warfare prayers as I was being tormented with condemnation; the condemnation then turned to depression.

I had never before experienced that type of depression. All I wanted to do was sleep; I had no energy to do anything. I even started taking over-the-counter sleeping pills, just so that I could sleep.

My two sons were little at the time, and I knew I had to take care of them. All I could do was drag myself to the store and buy a lot of T.V. dinners for them to eat. I did not have the strength to cook and could barely make it to work every day. I cried endlessly and began to have thoughts of dying. The pain and torment was so extreme that I felt it would be better for me to go to heaven and experience peace with Jesus Christ. I can remember muttering words such as *"Jesus, just take me."* The enemy was trying to get me to forfeit my destiny; the very thing I asked God for when I said yes.

The depression spiraled downwards. I felt as if I was on the brink of losing my mind; I am talking about "admit yourself in the hospital" type of losing your mind. Never in my life had I experienced such an attack on my sanity. It felt as if Satan himself had released a hoard of devils against me, and I didn't know how to defeat them on my own—the attack was too strong. Instead of admitting myself to the hospital, I called up an intercessor that I had met earlier that year to pray for me.

From the depths of my heart, I cried out to God to deliver me. When it became difficult to pray for myself, I would open the book of Psalms and read aloud. I became *desperate* for prayer from others because it was getting hard for me to pray for myself. I reached out to those that I knew would pray and war on my behalf. I had a colleague who was a woman of God and a spiritual mother to me. Some days, at work, I would have literal breakdowns, and thank God, she was available to pray for me. She would lay hands on me and pray for peace over my mind.

The depression, thoughts of dying and the threat on my sanity, then turned into physical torment. It was as if I was pregnant. Daily, I experienced morning sickness and would throw up like clockwork. I lost weight drastically. My church family, friends and those around me thought I was losing weight because I used to be on a weight loss program. When someone would comment on my weight loss, I would refer to that weight loss program. It was a good cover up. I was too embarrassed to share about what was really going on with me and I thought that the majority of people would not understand or believe what I was going through.

I finally went to the doctor. He·ran tests and found nothing wrong with me. However, he did diagnose that I was going through depression and prescribed some anti-depressives. I didn't like the thought of using medication to ease the depression and I refused to take them as he prescribed. However, one day, I became so desperate that I took half a tablet to feel some sense of relief. It mellowed me out. I thought, *"This is alright, I feel pretty good."* I decided to take half until I was totally delivered. By God's grace, I did not become addicted.

At the time, I needed physical intervention until my spiritual breakthrough came forth. Along with taking the medication, I was advised to take a natural herb called serotonin. Serotonin can aid with sleeping and mood regulation. However, I found that it made me drowsy for most of the time.

I went through this test and trial for six months. Every day, I listened to "You are my Peace" by Juanita Bynum. God gave me the strength to keep on praying and crying out to Him. During this time, the enemy himself came to me and said, "If you stop praying I will leave you alone." I came very close to giving up praying because the pressure was so strong, but I knew my prayers had to

63

be working, and the enemy's ultimate goal was to cause me to give up. I could see no way out but knew I had to fight for my boys.

I shed so many tears during this time that I got tired of crying—I had had enough. One day I came home, opened the book of Psalms and started declaring things over the enemy. I started speaking with boldness; it was nothing but the fire of the Holy Spirit. The Lord Jesus Christ told me, "Now you are fighting!"

This was the turning point. This was the point where the Light broke through the darkness and burnt the fog away.

When God brought me out of that storm, I gave birth to public intercession and the fruit of the Spirit. God told me that I would never go through anything like that again, and I believed Him—and still believe Him. Will I go through hurt? Yes, but nothing on that level.

But now, this is what the Lord says—
he who created you, Jacob,
he who formed you, Israel:
"Do not fear, for I have redeemed you;
I have summoned you by name; you are mine.
When you pass through the waters,
I will be with you;
and when you pass through the rivers,
they will not sweep over you.
When you walk through the fire,
you will not be burned;
the flames will not set you ablaze.
For I am the Lord your God,
the Holy One of Israel, your Savior;...
Isaiah 43:1-3

Throughout the storm, He never left my side. His Holy Spirit became my Comforter and my Counselor. God allowed me to go through the storm. He used it to develop and train me; He used it to transform me—He began my TransHERmation.

Chapter 9

TransHERmation: The Warrior in Me

He Called Me to Pray

I can remember praying and talking to God a lot as a young girl. I loved to commune with God, and praying for others came easily to me. It didn't stop as I reached my teenage years, and into adulthood I continued to pray, but I wasn't only praying for myself: I was praying for others. If there was a situation that someone was going through, or I heard about, my natural instinct was to pray on their behalf. I became so engaged in prayer that I began to identify myself with prayer, and started volunteering to pray for others when I would hear them speak about things in their lives. For example, one of my colleagues made a comment that she wanted a husband. The praying person that I am said, "I will pray for God to send you a husband.", and lo and behold, she met her husband six months later. When I would pray on behalf of others, my faith and belief was so strong; I was confident that God heard, and that He was going to answer favorably. To this day, when I pray on behalf of someone else, I know and believe that He hears and answers.

When I was a teen, I did not think of prayer as a ministry or anything that I could be doing for the Kingdom of God. At the church we attended growing up, we didn't have a prayer line where prophets or prophetic intercessors prayed over people. As a matter of fact, I had never heard of the word intercession or intercessor. I recall having a conversation with my mom and stepdad saying that I wished they had a ministry in the church where all you did was pray for people. I had no idea that that ministry existed in churches because I had not experienced it at our church. I felt that I had a gift of prayer—and I wanted it to be utilized as a ministry.

As I mentioned before, when I lived in Atlanta, I was prophesied over at the age of fourteen that God would use me to pray over others, and I could see things in them that others could not see. I did not dwell on that prophecy when it didn't come to pass at the time that I thought it would, but I kept praying.

In my twenties, my prayers started shifting into, *"Lord send me a husband, Lord I want this or that car, Lord I want this or that job."* My prayers started to become self-centered, and they were all about tangible possessions. Praying for a husband was my number one agenda... I had the timeframe of when I was going to get married, what he would look like, and the long list of characteristics that I wanted him to have. That is a whole other book by itself! I experienced so many of my prayers being answered for others, to the point where I was ready for my prayers to be answered.

However, it started upsetting me when some of the things that I had prayed for others would come to pass, but the same prayer request for myself would not come to pass. My thoughts were, *"What is going on Jesus?"* I did not know at the time that God was getting ready to call me to another level of intercession and prayer. My focus had been on asking and receiving tangible "in my face" blessings. There was a time in my life that I could cry to God—literally, and He would give me what I wanted. It was just like a spoiled child or baby that cries, and gets her own way. I started noticing that crying to God got His attention, and so that was my plan, *"Cry to Dad-*

dy, and He would give me my way." Just like a baby; a baby learns really quickly that all they have to do is cry or whine and you will be right there to rescue them.

Well, how many of you know that a baby does not and should not stay a baby? A baby grows and craves milk so that it will one day eat meat. God was calling me to grow up in prayer, and the things that I was praying for were not what God wanted to do or give me during that particular season of my life. He was calling me to grow-up and graduate from "babyhood."

During this time, an intercessory team was not in place at my church and therefore, there was no training regarding prayer and intercession available. In my eyes, I did not think anything was wrong with how I was praying. I did not know that there was a higher level of prayer. I was so accustomed to experiencing my prayers being answered for others that I began to treat God as if He was a genie. I believed that whatever I asked, I would get it because that was the desire of my heart. One of my Scriptures I quoted at that time was Psalm 37:4, "Take delight in the Lord, and He will give you the desires of your heart." I took that Scripture to heart. Whatever I desired, I thought I could get it because I was delighting myself in the Lord. At no time did I seek Him for the plan, purpose and desires that He had for my life. It was all about what Lakeea wanted. So many have twisted the Scripture around and have treated God like a genie because of it. It wasn't that God did not want to give me a husband or tangible things, but those things had become my idols—I was putting things before Him. Additionally, there is a time and season for everything. It just wasn't my time. Jesus wanted to teach me that the things that you can't see are more important than the things that you can see.

I am not saying that asking God for things is wrong or bad, and I am definitely not saying that you should not ask God for a husband. But your entire prayer life should not just be about you. It should be about asking Him to remove sin from your soul, heart and mind. Your prayers should be about wanting to be more intimate with Him, and to experience more of Him and less of you.

They should be about more of walking in His love, peace and joy; more of thanksgiving and worshipping Him for who He is; more of wanting His wisdom; and more of walking according to His Word. Your prayer life should be at a position of seeking His Will, and seeking Him on how to pray for a specific person or situation. It's like praying before you pray.

My teacher of prayer and intercession was the Holy Spirit and because I was still growing in prayer, and was new in my walk of submission to God, He had to take me on a journey to learn through the Holy Spirit. In the previous chapter, I talked about my journey through depression and spiritual warfare. The enemy tried to take me out mentally through depression—but God had a better plan. The Scripture tells me that ALL things work out for the good of those that are called according to His purpose. What the devil meant for bad, was turned around for the good.

My attack of depression led me to the Father's feet. I had no choice but to call out to Him. I had no choice but to pray His will for my life. It was no longer about having a husband, a fancy car or anything else materialistic for that matter because I had lost my joy and peace. I lost my ability to focus or think straight because my mind was consumed with the lies of the enemy. A spirit of confusion entered into my mind and soul, and I wanted to literally die. I had no hope because I could see no hope. If it was not for the working of the Holy Spirit, I would not have been able to press at His feet for deliverance.

The Holy Spirit is not just a figment of your imagination. The Holy Spirit is the third person of the Godhead; the Holy Spirit is God living on the inside of you. The Holy Spirit is a person that is there to assist you. The Holy Spirit is there to comfort you, to be your advocate, give you strength, reveal Truth to you, convict you of sin. He empowers you and gives commands. The Holy Spirit transforms you...

When you accept Jesus Christ into your life as your Lord and personal Savior, the Holy Spirit comes to live on the inside of you—your Assistant, while on Earth, is on the inside of you to help you overcome every trial, tribulation and obstacle that you would ever face on Earth.

Because Jesus Christ was Lord over my life, the working power of the Holy Spirit caused me to press past my feelings of depression. It was this tribulation of depression that awakened a new level of intercession, and an introduction to spiritual warfare. I would not have ever learned the magnitude of intercession, prayer and spiritual warfare if I had not been through the tribulation of depression.

Transformation in Prayer

My prayer life began to change instantly, and I was no longer focused on tangible things. My whole perception of life changed; even the way I viewed people. It was more about making sure I kept His peace, joy, love, and His mind. My heart began to grieve and ache for people that did not have God's love, joy or peace because I knew what that felt like. My compassion for the lost rose to a different level. I was not easily offended from this birthing process because my focus was on lost souls coming to know Jesus. My peace was literally stolen from me, and I was able to empathize with the lost—in a whole new way. My focus was taken off of the things of this world; I didn't care about the things of this world. My favorite saying became, and still is to this day—"I would live in a box on the corner, if that box had peace in it."

God allowed me to see and experience many prayers being answered because of my prayers to strengthen my faith. A stronger pursuit comes when you actually see your prayers being answered. It stirs up something on the inside of you to pray more, longer and harder. It's like getting recognized for being a great manager on your job or a great servant leader in your church.

Praise and results will sometimes cause you to go in a deeper pursuit of that thing. I truly believe that God was strengthening my spiritual muscles; my relationship with Jesus Christ was already established, and I already saw Him work in my life, and the life of others. There was no way that I was going back—I knew He was real. It didn't matter when I did not see the manifestation of my prayers as soon as I would have liked to—He had already demonstrated Himself to be real in my life

I was willing to keep pursuing Him by any means necessary. I want you to start looking at every trial and tribulation that you go through differently. Ask yourself this question—What is it that God is trying to birth out of me through this process, test or tribulation? Trials hurt, and they hurt bad. No one likes to go through pain; but trust me when I say that God is up to something in your pain. There are times when God does not share with you all of the details. When I was first going through depression, I had no idea that I was being trained for battle; that I was being trained to engage the enemy. I had no idea that He was teaching me a new level of prayer—through the pain. If I knew what He was up to, I probably would have tried to manipulate the process. Trust God in every area of your life—the good and the bad, because He is birthing a jewel out of you. Keep it moving queen, God got you! Pain produces TransHERmation!

Now may the God of peace,
who through the blood of the eternal covenant
brought back from the dead our Lord Jesus,
that great Shepherd of the sheep,
equip you with everything good for doing his will,
and may he work in us what is pleasing to him,
through Jesus Christ,
to whom be glory for ever and ever.
Amen.
Hebrews 13:20-21

Chapter 10

TransHERmation:
The Graceful Progress

From My Heart to Yours

TransHERmation has occurred throughout the different stages of my life. It did not happen overnight, and believe it or not, I am still transforming. We are all on a continual TransHERmation journey in our lives. It isn't always easy, but worth the perseverance and push. Once you become aware of who you are and who God called "you" to be, TransHERmation will begin to take place. It is His Will for you to be transformed.

Hebrews 10:14 "For by one sacrifice he has made perfect forever those who are being made holy." TransHERmation is about being made holy through God's transforming power in our lives.

This part of the book journeys through the lessons and insights that God has given me on those stages of my life. He has always had His hand upon me, even when I was lost in my brokenness and sin. As you walk with me, and God puts His finger on the areas that He wants to transform, know that He is with you and He is for you.

Romans 8:28-30 "And we know that in all things God works for the good of those who love him, who have been called according to his purpose. For those God foreknew he also predestined to be conformed to the image of his Son, that he might be the firstborn among many brothers and sisters. And those he predestined, he also called; those he called, he also justified; those he justified, he also glorified."

Before TransHERmation Begins

Determine in your mind that you are ready to transform, that you are ready to go to the next level and get out of that stuck place. Believe it or not, your destiny, your state-of-being, and your progress in life is determined by your mindset. Romans 12:2 says, "Do not conform to the pattern of this world, but be transformed by the renewing of your mind. Then you will be able to test and approve what God's will is—His good, pleasing and perfect will."

You must want to be free and leave that place of oppression. It is hard to imagine that freedom is for you, when you have always been in bondage or slavery and, truth be told, you do not want to be in bondage, but this is who you have been for so long. As a matter of fact, it's all you really know.

The dictionary defines bondage as slavery or involuntary servitude; the state of being bound by, or subjected to, some external power or control. The external power that is working overtime to control your mindset and progress in life is the enemy; the devil and his imps. He is the driving force that is keeping you oppressed. Oppression is defined as keeping someone in subservience and hardship, especially by the unjust exercise of authority; to cause someone to feel distressed, anxious, or uncomfortable. The devil wants to torment you in your mind. He wants to make you feel uncomfortable, anxious and distressed to the point that you are depressed, and have no life in you to move out of that state of mediocracy. Once you come under agreement with the enemy and his lies, you are now bound and enslaved—controlled. But, you do not have to remain bound and controlled. You can, and will, be free.

God gives us free will and the ability to choose, and He empowers us to choose—we *can* choose to be free. The enemy wants to keep you bound from knowing who you are in Christ. When you are under the influence of the enemy, you are not able to express the creativity of the Creator. The devil wants to keep you distracted within the boundaries of your limited capability.

Did you catch it? *"Limited capability."* God calls us, His people, to be enlarged and stretched beyond what our own capabilities can do or reach. Jesus stated in His Word that we would do greater works, which tells me that there is something that is on the inside of you—dreams, visions and creativity—that you or anyone else for that matter, has never seen. Do you know that the infinite Wisdom of God wants to bring forth those greater works out of you—the unimaginable?

A mind that is free in Christ, and ruled by Christ, is not held captive. God has so much in store for you that you are unable to perceive because of your oppressed mind-set, and the seeds of lies that the enemy tells you. Lies such as, *"You are not meant for greatness. You're not smart enough; and this is what you were created for—enslavement!"*

Like Pharaoh, the devil, wants to keep you in a box of limitations that will hinder you from reaching your ulti-mate Kingdom assignment on this earth. That spirit of pharaoh will brainwash you into believing that your ad-vancement will only come through serving him and his vision, instead of God's vision. Psalm 75:6-7 (*KJV*) states: "For promotion cometh neither from the east, nor from the west, nor from the south. But God is the judge; he putteth down one, and setteth up another."

When you have been enslaved in your mind, it is very hard for you to believe that you can write a book, obtain a degree, marry again, become an entrepreneur, flow in the gifts of the Spirit, be used by God for His Kingdom assignments, write a grant, sit at the table with kings and princes, or get promoted on your job—the list can go on and on.

Self-pity begins to take root in your thought life and you begin to play back the "shoulda-coulda-woulda's". Yes, I do believe we can miss out on opportunities, just like Esau traded his birthright and pleaded with tears to have his inheritance, but it was too late. Hebrews 12:16-17, "See that no one is sexually immoral, or is godless like Esau, who for a single meal sold his inheritance rights as the oldest son. Afterward, as you know, when he wanted to inherit this blessing with tears, he could not change what he had done." Just because an opportunity was missed, does not mean that life is over. It does not mean that God does not have more in store for you. It does not mean that He will not open new doors for you.

Just like Paul stated in Philippians 3:13-14, "Brothers and sisters, I do not consider myself yet to have taken hold of it. But one thing I do: Forgetting what is behind and straining toward what is ahead, I press on toward the goal to win the prize for which God has called me heavenward in Christ Jesus." We are to press on and look forward to what is ahead. Forget about the opportunities you missed and the relationships that walked out of your life. God has new opportunities and new relationships in store for you. Stop dwelling on those opportunities that you missed, and look ahead to the new.

Do you know that dwelling on the past dulls your discernment to recognize new opportunities and new relationships? Take a moment to think and ponder on that. *Dwelling on the past dulls your discernment to recognize the new.* This is a tactic of the enemy.

If he can keep your mind on things of the past, he can stop you from recognizing what God wants to do in your present and future. Dare to leave the past in the past, and just forget about it.

> "Forget the former things;
> do not dwell on the past.
> See, I am doing a new thing!
> Now it springs up; do you not perceive it?
> I am making a way in the wilderness
> and streams in the wasteland."
> Isaiah 43:18&19

I pray that everyone reading this book will be free from memory recall. I pray that there will be no recollection of the things of the past that are hindering their future. I pray that the Egypt-mindset to go back to that place of comfortability, will be null and void in Jesus' name.

Do not yearn to go back as the Israelites did, and wandered in the wilderness for forty years because of their disobedience, rebellion and complaining. They were slaves in Egypt, yet they desired to go back all because they did not have the food they were used to eating. In the wilderness, they ate manna and water. It was no more steak, shrimp, roast, salad, greens, macaroni, yams, tomatoes, potatoes, hogs, dogs and juice—that is my version. But Scripture says in Numbers 11:5-6, "We remember the fish we ate in Egypt at no cost—also the cucumbers, melons, leeks, onions and garlic. But now we lost our appetite; we never see anything but this manna!" God was testing their hearts by putting them on, what I call, a forced fast; to see if they would trust and obey Him even when they did not have the food they so desired. The Israelites proclaimed, "We lost our appetite!"

That is exactly what God wanted. He wanted them to lose THEIR appetite. He wanted to strip them of their carnal cravings and desires; strip them of the old. I believe God wanted to get the old taste out of their mouths, and strip them of the customs that they were used to, so that He could give them better—a land flowing with milk and honey. I believe God did not want them to take the old desires and cravings into the new place; He wanted them to expect, and want, something greater.

Have you been so used to something or a certain mindset, that it seemed strange to think that your Heavenly Father will have something greater in store for you? I have been there. I used to hear the words, "there is greatness on the inside of you, or God has great things for you." I often wondered what that meant. I still often wonder what the magnitude of His greatness looks like for me. Even as I write this book, I am getting my feet wet. The key is stepping out of the boat, and trusting Him. God will only share so much with you; and the rest He will keep a secret until it is time.

Beloved, if only you would taste and see that the Lord is good and that you are created in the image of God with a purpose that goes beyond your wildest dreams.

The definition of transformation is: a marked change in form, nature, or appearance. May the second half of this book bring about a TransHERmation within you. I pray that God will give you the courage to leave the old ways of thinking, and embrace all that He has in store for you.

Chapter 11

Understanding God as a Loving Daddy

Remember when I mentioned that I had never experienced the discipline of a father? My mother would always discipline me. I am not insinuating that mothers cannot discipline their children or should only be nurturers, but it is an authority that God has given specifically to a man. There is a governmental order in the family that God put in place. He created Adam first, not Eve. I want to share a bit about family and God's designated order of authority and anointing in a family.

Adam had an assignment from God to name the livestock, the birds in the sky and all of the wild animals. God trusted Adam to be a leader and to govern. The Hebrew meaning of "govern" is rule, dominion, authority. He released a vision to Adam by allowing him to name the animals, and then God created Adam a helpmate to assist him with carrying out the vision. God gave man the dominion and authority to be the head of the woman, and the household. The man established order; he set the order.

The rulership that God gave to the man was not a mean, overbearing, unkind or violent kind of rulership; but the kind of rulership that disciplines out of love, protects, and sets order for the good of all. God gave man the authority in the beginning, and when that is taken away, the spirit of disobedience and rebellion takes root.

When the earthly father is not present to establish that authority and rulership in the family, it becomes difficult to obey other earthly authorities—and even God Himself.

Proverbs 1:8, "Listen, my son, to your father's instruction and do not forsake your mother's teaching." Again, we see the father setting order, laying out the blueprint, and the mother carrying out what he instructed. I have noticed that in the book of Proverbs, it is the father giving advice to the children. Sons and daughters need a father, and it does not have to be a biological father. A man with the heart and wisdom of God can have a lasting effect on any child.

My stepdad was not wise at the time, and did not use his authority appropriately at times, but he was trying to set order in the home that I was not receiving because I had never received this from a father before. When a child lacks that firm foundation of authority, discipline and dominion, laid down by a loving and kind father from the beginning, it is going to take much love, kindness and relationship-building to establish authority and trust in their lives.

Jesus draws us with love and kindness. Jeremiah 31:3, "The Lord appeared to us in the past, saying: 'I have loved you with an everlasting love; I have drawn you with unfailing kindness'."

Jesus chose us. We did not choose Him, and in doing so, He had to draw us by His love. Before Jesus came on the scene, we were wandering about—lost, without a Shepherd. We were fatherless, so He had to woo us, by His tender mercies. When He first calls us, we are babies in Christ, and He treats us as such by pouring out His love on us and instructing us through the Holy Spirit.

Hosea 11:3-4, "It was I who taught Ephraim to walk, taking them by the arms; but they did not realize it was I who healed them. I led them with cords of human kindness, with ties of love. To them I was like one who lifts a little child to the cheek, and I bent down to feed them." When a child receives love, kindness, authority and instruction from his/her earthly father on a consistent basis, he/she is able to receive love, kindness, authority and instruction from his/her Heavenly Father.

A father cannot be inconsistent in a child's life and think that he will have influence, or authority, over that child, because a relationship has not been established. Relationship is established through consistency. Look at our Father in Heaven: "Every good and perfect gift is from above, coming down from the Father of the heavenly lights, who does not change like shifting shadows." (James 1:17). Our Father in Heaven is consistent. He does not change.

God's perfect will was for the earthly father to be a representation of Him on the earth; this establishes order in the Kingdom. Just like the husband should be the head of his household, our Heavenly Father and Jesus Christ should be first in our lives. Jesus Christ submits to God, and the husband should be submitting to Jesus Christ. Sin has crept in and removed the divine order of the family. I believe this is why the male is under so much attack. The enemy wants to destroy the influence and authority of the man. If he succeeds at doing this, then he has attacked an entire generation.

Perhaps as you are reading this book, you realize that you have not had an earthly father in your life that established a foundation of authority and influence accompanied with love and kindness. Don't be in despair—there is hope. Take note that *I emphasize love and kindness*. Everything we do should be driven by love. I too did not have a consistent father figure in my life, but that does not mean that all hope is gone. Jesus Christ is always available, and remember, He chose you—you did not choose Him.

John 15:16, "You did not choose me, but I chose you and appointed you so that you might go and bear fruit—fruit that will last—and that whatever you ask in my name the Father will give you."

Since Jesus Christ chose you, then His love is available to you. His will, instruction and authority of the Father is available to you. He will not leave you as an orphan nor forsake you like your earthly father. He forgives you when you go to Him and confess your sins from a sincere heart. He then releases His grace and mercy upon you. This is why He shed His blood, so that you could have access to the Father's love; so that you could freely come to Him without fear of death; without fear of being condemned. You are only condemned when you reject Him, and when you reject the love that He is extending in your life.

John 3:18, "Whoever believes in him is not condemned, but whoever does not believe stands condemned already because they have not believed in the name of God's one and only Son."

There is no need to measure up, or feel like He is sitting back waiting on you to mess up so that He can condemn you. No. His agenda is to save you and set you free from the bondage of fear; the fear of trusting in Him. You don't have to fear trusting in Him because He truly loves you and thinks good of you and not evil. Jesus wants us to prosper—He does not have hidden motives. The devil wants you to believe this lie so he can keep you on his team, but his lies have been exposed.

Jesus died to cover the shame and guilt of sin; you no longer have to feel ashamed because a loving father always wants what is best for His child. He will discipline His child, protect His child, provide for His child, comfort His child, teach His child, and impart wisdom in His child. It doesn't always feel good to be disciplined, but it is for our good.

When we are able to meditate on the words, "He thinks good of me and not evil", then we are able to serve Him wholeheartedly—without the fear of being cast out of His sight.

I believe one of the devil's strategic plans to keep us away from our Heavenly Father's love, is to put a false representation of a father in our lives; put an inconsistent father in our lives, or the absence of a father altogether. Satan's objective or goal is to distort our thinking and relationship with our Heavenly Father.

What tends to happen is we treat our relationship with our Heavenly Father according to the relationship we had, or did not have, with our earthly father. Satan has a plot to create dysfunction in the family unit from the beginning because our foundation determines the course of our lives until we are free from Satan's grip.

My Steps to Realizing the Father Heart of God

- Knowing the heart of the Father is not being passive. I had to make a conscious decision to seek after God with all my heart, mind and soul, which means it takes sacrifice. I became consistent with fasting and prayer. Fasting and prayer open you up to a greater intimacy with Jesus Christ. When you earnestly seek Him, He begins to reveal more and more of who He is and how He feels about you.

- I had encounters with Jesus Christ through prayer. One of my visions during a prayer at church was Jesus Christ holding me in His arms. Right after I had this vision, someone came up to me and wrapped their arms around me and said, "Jesus is holding you in His arms." My God, this was the vision that I just had! Ask God for an encounter with Him to feel His peace and presence, or a vision to know that He accepts you as His own.

- Reading the Bible helped me, but I had to take it a step further and read other books that talked about the Father's heart and Grace. I needed to be reminded of the Love of the Father through the spirit of Grace, and the Power of the Blood of Jesus!

My Prayer for You

Dear Heavenly Father, I thank you for the woman of God that is reading this prayer. I thank you Lord that she is experiencing and receiving the love of the Father. I thank you Lord that you will never leave her nor forsake her. I thank you Lord that she sees her worth in You – the Father! I thank you Lord that she is experiencing divine encounters with You that lets her know that you are Daddy. Thank you Lord that she can cry out Abba Father, without the fear of being rejected by You. Lord I thank you that she is no longer in bondage to fear. I thank you Lord that she is not an orphan, but she belongs to You. Thank you Lord that she is receiving divine revelations from You. Lord I thank you that she is experiencing you in a more intimate way! Thank you, Jesus, that she knows the heart of the Father and that she is walking in complete freedom. Thank you Lord for healing the deep wounds of hurt for her not experiencing the love of her earthly father. Lord, I thank you that she has forgiven her earthly Father. Lord, I thank you that she is walking in complete forgiveness, healing and deliverance. In Jesus' Name, Amen!

Chapter 12

The Teenage Years: Painful Lessons

In my teenage years, the bottled up and suppressed hurt that I had from childhood began to cause me to be in consistent conflict with my mom. The deep wounds of hurt caused me to act out destructively. I grew up seeing and hearing a lot of abuse; therefore, I had not been shown a positive way to handle hurts and frustrations. Having decent conversations was not something that was normal in our household; it was mainly yelling. All the hurt and anger that I had caused me to even reject my mother's affection. I resisted it at all costs as a teen; it was even hard for me to say, "I love you" at times.

As a little girl, especially after my parents divorced, and we moved to my grandmother's house, I openly received affection from my mom. I remember her giving me a hug and kiss every night, and us telling each other that we love each other. Something took a turn when my mom remarried, and I believe it was the suppressed feelings of rejection and abandonment from my father that manifested in me that brought the conflict. When I entered my teenage years, I really began to rebel against my mother. I had no respect for her, and words of discipline or grounding me no longer worked. I talked back to my mom, and we were in constant conflict with each other.

During my pre-teen and especially my teenage years, I did not feel comfortable talking to my mom about personal things or my true feelings because I knew the response I would get. My mom was old school—she did not play, and there were some things that I knew not to talk to my mom about because I knew how she felt about it. For example, going to my mom about wanting to be on birth control because I wanted to start having sex, was an automatic mouth lashing. Those types of conversations were too devastating for my mother to hear her daughter talk about.

My daddy, on the other hand, was the opposite. I could approach him about anything, and he was going to talk to me as if he was talking to a friend and would keep it real with me. He wasn't easily moved in his emotions by the things that I would say; he was more understanding. I was more apt to open up to my daddy because I didn't feel condemned.

Words of Wisdom to Parents with Teens

I believe that once a teenager feels singled out or rejected, it is hard to fully gain the intimacy of the relationship back. When a teenager feels that they cannot trust you or be open and honest with you without feeling condemned and judged, they will instantly close up and will be reluctant to share anything with you. Most of the time, they will share little to nothing with you.

If you have a teenager that will not talk to you or open up to you regarding concerns or issues, it may be because of how you make him or her feel when you do talk to them. What is your approach? Oftentimes parents think that the disciplinarian approach that was successful as a child, will work as a teenager. However, when kids reach the teen years, a sudden shift begins to happen and you can no longer use the same approach.

This is why it is so important to train a child when they are young, but sometimes even training a child in the right way when they are young, doesn't always stop mis-behaviors and rebellion. There are developmental stages, and your teenager is no longer your baby or the child that you once raised. They have now seen, or even ex-perienced, things that they never have before; and a lot of times peer pressure and their curiosities have opened them up to sex, drugs and whatever else. I was moved by peer pressure as a teenager, but I also did not have that open communication and relationship with my mom.

A teenager that feels any rejection or abandonment from either parent is not going to be open about what they are going through. Please do not get it twisted. In the case that your teenager does open up to you, it does not mean that he/she will not make mistakes or go through growing pains. We must remember that we were once young teenagers too and probably gave our parent(s) a hard time. If you did not, then your parent(s) were blessed!

Having the ability and skill of empathy with a teenager is the best way to gain that trust again. It will take time, consistency and persistence. You need to have a level of understanding and discernment of the deep-rooted is-sues your teenager is going through. Knowing the reason behind the reason (behavior) will give you greater pa-tience and wisdom in handling your teenager. I am sure my mom wanted the best for me, but couldn't get past my negative behaviors and acting out episodes, especial-ly the deliberate disobedience. My behaviors were being given more attention than the deep-rooted issues that were the reason behind the behavior.

The reason I did not feel loved at times, and felt like I was misunderstood, was because I was always being scolded, and was not able to express myself without feel-ing condemned. The signal that you are sending a teen-ager when you revert to yelling, condemning and punishment is "You are not loved, or you are not understood" and they will receive the signal of *"I am not loved or I am not understood."*

If you are experiencing this, I hope this is making sense to you. I can hear a parent saying, "Nah just knock him or her out; nah you ain't gonna be acting like that with me" and so on. I understand what you are saying, but the fact that I was that rebellious, disobedient teenager, I can relate to how they are feeling. The negative behaviors are definitely behaviors that warrant correction; however, you must, *I repeat, you must use wisdom*, and pray to God for that wisdom in dealing with your teenager.

I will say this—no one is given a manual for parenthood, and you will make mistakes. Not every parent is aware that there are some deep-rooted issues going on with their children; the reason for the rebellion and disobedience. I made similar mistakes with my teenage boys until I caught the revelation. I caught the revelation and asked God for wisdom in how to deal with my sons. I asked Him how to respond to their negative behaviors or decisions they made that I did not agree with. Let me tell you, it made a world of a difference. Don't be so quick to count them out; just like the devil is after your purpose, he is after theirs, and we must fight for them through prayer.

If you are a single mother, do not try to do it alone, get a support system that will encourage you and impart wisdom. And, do not be so self-righteous that you will not get your child help if they so need it. As I stated, if your teenager does not feel that they can trust you, or they feel rejected or abandoned, he/she is not going to open up to you. It's okay to get outside help from a professional Christian counselor, Christian psychologist or pastor. Do not wait until your child turns eighteen when you do not have any control over them getting help.

I also advise you to take your son or daughter to get deliverance from deep wounds of hurt. My rebellion was out of rejection, abandonment and deep hurt. It's a process, and he or she will overcome!

On Mentoring Teens

During my teenage years in Battle Creek, there was nothing going on for the youth. No one establishing programs or activities; we barely had a bowling alley and skating rink. All of us that hung out together, had the same things on our mind—sex, smoking weed, drinking, playing cards, hanging out at each other's houses and joy riding. No one was talking about owning a business, writing a book, going to church, being an entrepreneur, attending college or anything else along those lines. I am not saying that opportunities were not available to me or existed back then, but what I am saying is, it was not something that was made visible to me. I didn't have a coach or mentor that invested in me.

It is so easy for people to say what should or shouldn't be done about the teens of today—but talk is cheap. We must be action-orientated people. It's not enough to talk about the issues and problems that exist in our communities if we are not willing to do something about it. We should be willing to take in a teenager, or mentor them, coach them, show love, encourage and support them. It is about getting your hands dirty to help your community advance.

I want to pose a question to you. What are you doing to help your community? What are you doing to help someone less fortunate than you? Are you willing to invest your time and energy in someone else? It is easy to blame but we must be a solution. My life would have possibly had a different direction if someone had coached and mentored me with wisdom and grace through the teenage years.

My Steps to Communicating with Teenagers

- I had to pray for God's wisdom on communicating with my teenagers. Every teenager is different, with a different personality, and it's not always going to be the same.

- Pray for God's wisdom and trust His leading.

My Prayer for You

Dear Heavenly Father, I thank you for the woman of God reading this prayer with teenagers, and even if she does not have teenagers and reading this prayer, I thank you for her heart to be an encouragement and positive influence to teenagers. Lord I thank you that you are giving her the wisdom that she needs to communicate with her teenagers and every teenager that she encounters or connected to. I thank you Lord that she is correcting and disciplining out of love and not anger. I thank you Lord that she is not provoking her child to anger, but walking in the wisdom of God when it comes to her teenager. Lord, I thank you that every teenager that she is connected to, including her own, is covered by the blood of Jesus, and protected by the angels all the days of their lives. I thank You that they are walking in their purpose, and not influenced by the things of this world that will distract them from walking in their divine purpose. Lord, I thank you for breaking the spirit of sabotage that would come through people or situations to stop them from walking the path that you have for their lives. I thank you Lord that they are returning to the God of their youth, and for those that never knew you, I pray that salvation will knock at their hearts, and they will let you in. I thank you for bringing other mentors and coaches in their path to minister and counsel them on the Word of God, walking in their purpose, and avoiding wrong relationships. We thank you Lord that they have discerning hearts that know right from wrong and they are avoiding every path of destruction. Thank you Lord for connecting them to the right relationships, and disconnecting them from the wrong ones. We thank you Lord for the strength for the mother reading this prayer. Thank you Jesus, that you hear her prayers regarding her teenager. Thank you Lord for lifting every burden she carries and removing the spirit of heaviness off of her heart. Thank you Jesus, that you are her comfort and peace. Thank you Jesus, that she and her teenager(s) has victory through you. In Jesus' Name, Amen!

Chapter 13

My Experience as a Young Mother: Beautiful and Painful

As a teen mother, all attention is on you because, for one, you are way too young to be having a child. You are still developing and most of the time you do not fully know who you are.

The first time I fell pregnant, I was sixteen years old. I did not plan on falling pregnant—that was not on my agenda or plans. I was attracted to this young man that was at my high school, and a lot of girls liked him. It always felt good to have the guy that all the girls were attracted to, like you. Most of the time in high school, the one that all the girls liked was also a player, but that didn't matter. All that mattered was, I was being paid attention to and someone found me attractive.

Growing up, I didn't feel too attractive, which watered the seed of rejection. I wasn't affirmed by my father either or shown the ropes when it came to boys; what to avoid or what to do. It was easy for me to fall in the trap of being pursued by the wrong guy, especially if they were attractive and found me to be attractive. It was all about attraction as a teenager. I didn't have a clue about the importance of a gentleman; the importance of him not being promiscuous or a player; or the importance of education.

The enemy will deceive you with the superficial, in order to cloud your thinking and blind your eyes to what is real. The enemy desensitizes your discernment of knowing what is right, and the more your flesh is fulfilled, the more you are deceived. You drift further away from the truth—become blinded to the truth. The more you are deceived and blinded, the more you begin to operate in rebellion.

As a teenager, I became desensitized to the truth and I operated in rebellion. The hollowness from rejection was being temporarily filled by wrong relationships, and the attention I longed for, was only superficially satisfied by those relationships. I was still trying to fulfill that empty void inside of me, and I thought that a baby would completely fill it. I couldn't perceive that I was opening myself up to even more traps of the enemy...

Teen Pregnancy

Teen pregnancy is prevalent in single parent homes. When there is an imbalance of two active parents in a child's life, then the child is missing out on what is needed to be a whole person. A child needs a mother and a father. A lot of brokenness in society is because of this lack; either the father was/is missing out of the home or child's life, or the mother was/is missing out of the child's life.

The father plays a prominent role (as mentioned previously), but a broken person can come from either an absent parent because both parents have an important role to play in that child's life. The mother is the nurturer, caregiver and teacher of the instructions that the father lays out for the family. The father carries the authority as the head of the household, provides direction, protects, imparts, leads the family spiritually and provides for his family financially. Both parents provide love and kindness—but out of distinct roles. The love of a father is different to the love of a mother, and both play a vital part in the child's life.

When there is dysfunction in a family, and a lack of either parent, the child or teen will seek to fill that void elsewhere—hence the prevalence of teen pregnancy in those single parent homes. However, even though the teenager commits an act of fornication and makes a "life mistake" by seeking love out of marriage, the pregnancy is not a mistake—life is never a mistake. God has intent and purpose for that conception and the precious life that is there.

The Lord does what He wants to do and how He wants to do it. We did not choose our parents, but God ordained our parents to be our parents for a reason and a purpose. There is a purpose behind everything that God does, and He ultimately gets the glory.

I was young when I had my sons: eighteen and twenty-one, but their birth gave life to me re-focusing on the plans and purposes God had for my life. God caused my thinking to shift from off myself to my children. I am not in any way saying that you should purposely go out and commit fornication or any such sin so that God can get the glory. I was ignorant and did not know God in the way that I know Him now. I was blinded and deceived, yet God was able to get the glory out of what the enemy was trying to destroy. Yes, there were setbacks; and consequences, but my pregnancies did not allow me to stay in a stuck place. God brought me through!

Overcoming teen pregnancy was a choice that I made by God's Grace. My situation was a little different to some teenage mothers because I had my own apartment, my own car and a job. I demonstrated responsibility. The key to overcoming any mistake in life is to take the focus off yourself. You were put here to be the deliverer of someone else. Once I had children, I wanted to build a stable future for them and be a role model to them; an example of a productive citizen in society.

If you are in a place of stagnation because of some wrong decisions you have made, I challenge you to think about those that need you. Believe it or not, there are people that are assigned to you, and your children are definitely assigned to you. Every decision that you make, should be with them in mind, and that includes grandchildren too.

The Bible speaks on leaving an inheritance for your children's children. I challenge you to start; to move forward and to dream again. Seek God on the plan and purpose that He has for your life, for your children, grandchildren and anyone else that is connected to you. Do not be like Jonah, and refuse to walk in the things of God. There have been plenty of times that I wanted to give up and walk away from this saved life in Christ because of the trials and tribulations, but then I would look at the trials, tribulations and struggles of my boys, and know that I could not afford to give up because giving up on myself would mean giving up on them.

When you decide to give up on doing the right things and living for Jesus Christ, you are giving up on the deliverance of others; you are giving up on the breakthroughs of others. Your children, grandchildren, family, friends, leaders, and even your enemies need your prayers. Your children and family need you to return to school, start that business, write that book, operate in your Kingdom gifts and talents—whatever they might be. God did not create you to live on this earth to drink, play and be merry. He did not create you to be mediocre or average. He created you for a Kingdom assignment that goes beyond what you can see right now!

He created you to be someone's answer. It doesn't matter what your talent or gift is; it was created to be the answer for someone, to be a blessing to someone. If you know how to do hair, God gave you that talent to do other people's hair; to provide hair care; to make women feel good about themselves. I don't know what I would do without my hairdresser. I want you to know that it doesn't matter what God called you to do; it is ALL ministry unto Him; at least it should be. The next time you want to allow a trial or tribulation to cause you to give up, think about this, *"I have potentially given up on my children, family, friends, church family or maybe even an entire nation."*

God may have told you that you are called to the nations; therefore, your voice, talent or gift is going to impact millions of people, but if you stop here, they will not be able to experience what only "you" can offer them. There is only one handprint like yours; therefore, you have been fearfully and wonderfully made to touch the people or a situation that is assigned specifically to you. It just may be your prayer, your smile or encouraging word that is going to cause them to be delivered. Do not be selfish. God requires us to be givers—givers of our time, talent, gifts, money, and possessions. What you have, is for someone else, to bless that person.

I love to challenge people, and I am challenging you to think about a person or persons, and if you have children, think about your children. Think about the purpose that God has for their lives. Begin to see the tests, trials and tribulations they are facing. Begin to see how the devil is trying to wreak havoc in their lives or trying to stop their purpose. Once you do that, make a decree that you will not let your past failures affect your present or future because you have lives that you are responsible for. Imagine if we all thought that way. I believe this is a part of what God means when He says, "Esteem others better than yourselves." Think of others more highly than yourself. Think of their present and future more highly than your own. Philippians 2:3: "Do nothing out of selfish ambition or vain conceit. Rather, in humility value others above yourselves." This Scripture clearly says that it's not about you. They have a destiny to fulfill, now pick yourself up and forward march!

My Steps to Persevering Through Teen Pregnancy

- **Focus on others**: It's simple: I took my mind off me and put it on the lives that God entrusted to me.

- **I went into pursue mode**. I needed to have a dream and vision for my life. I needed to take the necessary steps to make sure my children had a comfortable and stable life. I signed up for trade school and then later pursued my degree.

- **It is important to have vision for your future**. If you do not know, begin to pray and ask God what His plans are for your life and what goals can you pursue right now to have a better life for yourself and children. There are some long-term dreams and aspirations that you have for your life that will take some time to obtain; but there are some immediate changes that can take place in your life. Getting an education was my goal because I needed to do something to get out of the factory. Maybe going to college or trade school is not for you, get a mentor or coach that can aid you in obtaining some goals that will bring results. You have a huge part to play in that; you cannot expect your coach or mentor to do the work for you, but they will give you wise counsel and aid you to the necessary resources.

- **I had a support system**. I was young with children and needed a support system. My mom and stepdad were my biggest supporters. It really does take more than you to raise your child, but make sure the right people are in your life helping you with your children. As parents, we are to protect our children and allowing any and everybody around them is a no-no!

- **I disconnected myself from negativity**. Negativity is a distraction! Bad company corrupts good manners, and you are raising kings and queens!

My Prayer for You

Dear Heavenly Father, I thank you for the woman of God reading this prayer. Lord I thank you that she is not distracted by life's obstacles. I thank you that she is continuing to press forward no matter what. Lord, I thank you that she is completely trusting in you to work out everything for her good. Lord, I thank you that she is not giving up on You or her divine purpose and destiny. Lord, I thank you that she is moving forward in her God-given purpose, both spiritually and physically—no matter what that purpose may be. I thank you Lord that she is disconnecting herself from every toxic—negative relationship that would prevent her from moving forward in her God-given purpose. I thank You that she is esteeming others better than herself. I thank you Lord that you are blessing the works of her hands and that the works of her hands are blessing others; especially her children, spouse, family and even a nation. Lord, I thank you that her prayers are causing deliverance, healing and breakthroughs in others. Lord, I thank you that she is remaining in position and staying in a posture of prayer. Lord, I thank you that nothing is stopping her worship towards you. Lord, I thank you that she is not growing weary in well-doing. I thank you Lord that her labor is not in vain and that she is reaping a harvest for her faithfulness. In Jesus' Name, Amen!

Chapter 14

The Demonic Spirits of Abandonment and Rejection

Abandon: Cast away, leave, or desert.
Reject: Dismiss as inadequate, unacceptable, or faulty.

How many of you know that when you have experienced something for a long time, it becomes normal to you? It is also said that you don't miss something that you have never before experienced or had.

The lack of a consistent father figure in my life caused me to have many hidden and suppressed emotions in my heart. Because of these suppressed and hidden emotions, I was under the influence of a number of spirits. There was a hidden spirit of abandonment and also the spirit of rejection—abandonment and rejection go hand-in-hand.

When one is living your everyday life, moving forward and coping fairly well, it is hard to believe or identify an issue that you may have. This was me! I was used to coping without having my father in the same household or having him in my life on a consistent basis; it was normal, and I did not love him any less. I continued to respect, honor and visit my daddy from time-to-time. I dismissed his dysfunction as "that's just how he is." How many times do we do that as a people? We dismiss dysfunction as "normal" because that is how a person has always been, and we make statements such as "that's just how they are." When in fact "how they are", can very well be a demonic spirit that is having influence over their lives.

I had a hidden demonic spirit of abandonment that opened the door for me to seek affection from the wrong type of men. I thought it was "just the way I am." I did not realize that the hidden spirit of abandonment was causing me to gravitate towards the affection of men, and the wrong type of men.

Side note: Ladies, be careful of giving your heart to someone that you clearly are not engaged to or married to. A sidekick or a man who has shown no interest in marrying you, should not get your whole heart. I'm not talking about mere words of "I love you" or "I am going to marry you one day." No. It needs to be a demonstration of love. This is why it is so important to have Jesus Christ as the head of your life to lead and guide you—to inform you of the counterfeits; but we all know that is not always the case, and not always easy to hear Him because most of the time we are searching for love in all the wrong places.

I gave so much love, and wanted to receive an abundance of love in return. I had an empty void of abandonment, and the attention and false affection from men satisfied my flesh. The spirit of abandonment caused me to place my value in others, and base my self-worth on their opinion of me. I was moved by whether they liked me or not—I would become consumed in my emotions or thoughts if I thought a person did not like me or accept me for who I am.

As I mentioned at the beginning of this chapter, I was also dealing with rejection, which I had from when I was in my mother's womb. Throughout my life, rejection and abandonment have simultaneously influenced me. When my parents divorced, it was as if my dad divorced me too—I felt the rejection and abandonment, but didn't recognize it at the time. I just suppressed it—and hid it. When my mom remarried, I felt like the outcast. Not only did I not like the idea of my mom remarrying, but I did not like to be part of family vacations or family moments.

I would walk far behind my family, keep a frown on my face, and engage in as little conversation as possible. I would act out rejection and abandonment without always having a reason to. Abandonment and rejection caused me to do so many things that I normally wouldn't have done—just to receive acceptance. Rejection caused me to put myself in a potential harm's way—just to be accepted.

Let me explain how rejection started in my mother's womb. One day, while going through a deliverance session, I asked the Holy Spirit where rejection first entered in, and He revealed to me that my mother experienced rejection when she was pregnant with me, and what she was feeling transferred to me. The enemy already has a heads up with us when we are conceived. He sets up death threats and every tactic he can to get us off course. I already had the spirit of rejection on the inside of me, and as you can remember from the beginning of this book, I experienced my first rejection in my first week of school, when the other kids made fun of my hairstyle.

It doesn't feel good to be talked about or ridiculed, so to avoid that from happening, you make sure that you are on your "A" game and you are "fitting in." This is an open door for another spirit—the spirit of perfectionism. Those that are perfectionists, are people pleasers and place their value in what people think of them. I struggled with this throughout my life too.

It is hard for a rejected person and a perfectionist to take constructive criticism and correction, because correction is now perceived as, *"You have a problem with me."* or *"I must not be good enough."*—when that is not the case at all. The Bible says that a wise person takes correction, but a foolish person does not. A person experiencing rejection, abandonment and perfectionism is also easily offended.

If you want to check if you are healed or delivered from these spirits, pay attention to how you respond to correction, how you respond when you are talked about, or if you are easily offended.

Being oversensitive is another clue that there is some rejection there and possibly abandonment issues. I was that person. I didn't want to be that person, but did not know how to overcome it. A rejected and abandoned individual will automatically assume that a person thinks the worst of them without even knowing what that person is actually thinking. It is hard for a rejected person to receive compliments, especially if they have grown up being called names or have experienced many losses or betrayals from those that they love or have loved dearly.

Just Be You—Who You Were Created to Be

Someone that is shy by nature, struggles with who they are as a person, and therefore struggles with rejection. They reject themselves and they fear the rejection from others—opening the door to fear. Growing up, I was always shy. I didn't want to approach anyone at all. I didn't want to be up front in the limelight; and I would feel extremely uncomfortable when someone would speak highly of me. I did not equate this to rejection. I knew it was a part of fear, but not rejection.

I didn't think I was good enough and often compared myself to others that appeared to be doing better than me, which is insecurity. I was insecure in my own abilities, and in who God created me to be. I judged the uniqueness of who God created me to be based on what someone else thought. For example, I loved to laugh and joke around, and if there was a bitter-serious person that would give me the look...you know the look, like, *"All that laughing is not called for"* it would cause me to draw back and keep a guard over how much laughter or how much of myself I would demonstrate around that person. I would adjust and hide the uniqueness of who God created me to be around those that misunderstood me; those that were too uptight, or too bitter. I judged my value based on their interaction, or even their non-verbal reaction towards me. I didn't want to be disliked or an outcast. I was willing to hide my true self behind a mask in order to pacify others and to feel accepted.

Until one day God told me, "Do not stop being who you are because of others' insecurities." A light bulb went off... Drop the mic! They were experiencing many of the same issues, but it came off as a bitter, snooty, and a *"who does she think she is"* type of attitude towards me. Those that had a problem with me being me were actually insecure about themselves and jealous of my security in being myself. I also often felt that way when I dressed up. I felt that others would judge me. I come from a family of dressers—it's in our blood, and I often wanted to make sure that I wasn't doing too much because of what someone may think about it, but again the Holy Spirit said, "Do not let their insecurities stop you from being who I created you to be."

If you are drawing back from walking in the fullness of who God called you to be because of someone else's opinion of you, know that their opinion is based on their own insecurities and issues. Do not hold people's opinion in high regard that do not have a say over your life. Jesus Christ holds all authority—He is the one that created you. How dare you allow someone to have so much control and authority over your life that you stop being who you are.

Look at how many inventors and famous people are totally "out of the box" with their look, their brand, speech and ideas. There are millionaires and billionaires that are doing it. They dared to be their unique selves.

What if they decided to hide behind their uniqueness because of what others may say or think, the looks they would get, or because they are trying to please people? They would not be where they are today if they had listened to those fears.

When abandonment and rejection are not dealt with, you are not fully able to be your authentic self. Abandonment and rejection are designed to put limitations on you. This is why the enemy likes to get you young so that way, the spirit can get so rooted in you that you are not able to associate with your true identity. People that are going through abandonment and rejection issues have a deep desire to be loved, and flattering words of manipulation can easily deceive a wounded, abandoned and rejected individual.

I always felt bamboozled by men because they were presenting themselves one way, and over time ended up being someone totally different. I was easily manipulated. I often experienced letdowns and heartbreaks from people that I showed a genuine love for and interest in. This opened up the door to me feeling suspicious of those who would come into my life and try to get close to me. I became very hesitant of people's motives because every time I would let someone in, they would break my heart, manipulate me or use me in some form or fashion. I had to realize that I could not continue life like that and to trust God to bring the right relationships into my life. I had to learn the skill of praying about things first instead of afterwards.

Pray that God will send you genuine friends and the right mate. Pray that God will protect you from those that mean you no good. You have to know and trust that God has your back when it comes to relationships. I believe there are some relationships that God will allow you to experience in order to grow and strengthen you for your next season. Some relationships He needs you to experience to work some things out of you. For example, love, patience and kindness. God tells us to love our enemies and to do good to them, so how can you do good to an enemy, if He never puts one in your life? Everything works out for the good of those that are called according to His purpose. Pray and ask God for discernment in all things. Do not miss out on your actual blessings because you are so suspicious of people.

I am not saying connect with any and everybody that comes into your life or tries to befriend you, but definitely have wisdom and pray. Even Jesus was only in a close intimate relationship with twelve disciples, and out of the twelve there were three that He was closely knit to. Therefore, you are not called to everybody.

Another revelation out of that is that Jesus' friends are those that are in intimate relationship with Him; those that follow Him and obey His commands. You definitely want your team to be those that support you and your vision. Are you celebrated by those that are on your team? Are you encouraged? Will they be totally honest with you, even if it hurts? Is the relationship reciprocal, or are you the only one giving and giving, while they are taking and taking? These are some questions to ask yourself as you enter into intimate relationships.

Without question, you should be equally yoked with those that you are in relationship with. Dark and light have nothing in common. It is a different story when you are winning souls and in relationship with unbelievers; to be a light, and to be a witness, but to engage in their activity is a no-no.

The Beginning of Walking in Freedom

My fears of abandonment and rejection started to carry over into my relationship with Jesus. I always feared that He was angry with me when I messed up. I had this idea that He was a hard father that would be upset with me if I made mistakes. The wrong mindset and concept of God will tell you that He is mad at you and will not accept you unless you work your way to heaven—it dismisses the friendship and relationship with Jesus Christ.

The wrong mindset will tell you that, "If I do not jump up and down three times, turn around, slap my neighbor, pray five hours a day, and fast with only water, then I am not saved or in relationship with Jesus Christ."

I am exaggerating, but you get the picture. I have been there, not to that extreme, but definitely in bondage to working my way to heaven, without a true loving relationship with my heavenly Father, to the point where condemnation would set in because I did not feel I was worthy to be called His daughter.

Jesus wanted to shift my thinking to look at Him as a loving "Daddy" and not a dictating father. Did you catch the word *"Daddy"*? You see, Jesus knows that Daddy is more intimate to me; it is more of a loving, caring, free relationship that a daughter has with her father. "Daddy" speaks to my heart because there is affection and a nurturing relationship that a daddy has with his daughter—"Daddy" is a friend and protector. Yes, Daddy disciplines his daughter because He loves her. He does not turn His back on His daughter because she makes mistakes or messes up from to time to time.

When I was in prayer one evening, God imparted this truth in me by showing me a vision of me in an open field, skipping, twirling, and spinning around; it was as if I was a child. Jesus was in the field with me. As a child has no worries, fears, stress or burdens, I had no care or worry—my complete trust was in Him. I was free and safe because I was with my Daddy. During this vision from my Heavenly Father, I knew that He was showing me that I was His little girl, His daughter. There is such a pureness of heart when you are a child. At that moment, I knew that He truly looked upon my heart and could see the tenderness of a child. It also reminded me of the Scripture Matthew 18:3, "And he said: Truly I tell you, unless you change and become like little children; you will never enter the kingdom of heaven." Children are very trusting and full of faith, and depend on their parents for everything. I know this is what my Daddy wanted me to know, "Trust and depend on Me totally. It is in this place that you will experience great freedom, peace and joy."

The impartation from my Daddy that evening was so real that it caused me to refocus my thinking. How *He* felt about me is what truly mattered, not how I felt about myself or even how others felt about me. I felt with confidence that I had my Daddy's heart and He had mine; a peace consumed me that brought uncontrollable tears to my eyes. It was in this moment that TransHERmation firmly took root because I was finally secure with who God created me to be in His image.

We are all uniquely made—His very own masterpiece. He is the Creator of creation; therefore, He is expressed differently through every one of us. He does not express Himself in the same way. He made you who you are for His purpose, and He wants to express the creativity of His glory through you. He has a sound that He wants to express through you. He has a sermon, prayer, painting, dance, song, witty idea, invention, or whatever talent or gift that He wants to express through you. People are very good at comparing themselves with others, but you are only anointed in who God created you to be. How can you be effective trying to imitate or be someone else other than who God called you to be? It is called a fake or counterfeit anointing. I often felt different because of how God used me, and worried about what others thought of me because of it. I often felt misunderstood and lonely, but to God be the Glory for that vision He gave me. It literally freed me from the deception that I was not good enough.

I had conditioned myself to believe that God was not pleased with me. Talk about bondage. Instead of me running to Him and talking to Him as a friend and loving Father—I ran from Him. Instead of emptying myself before Him, I would wallow in self-pity, until He gave me the realization that He does love me and accepts me and my flaws.

He loves you and your flaws too! Do not get me wrong. I'm not saying that you are exempt from repenting before God and asking for forgiveness, or exempt from living a holy life. But what I am saying is He accepts you right where you are. He is the only One that can clean those flaws up and create the precious diamond and jewel that you are.

I was that person that did not believe that God accepted me and that His love for me is truly unconditional. I was that person that was in bondage and oppressed— enslaved in an Egypt mindset. I did not believe that I was good enough to accomplish things on an above average level.

My thoughts were often, *"Who me, not me, and even why me."* I could not see myself being used by God for a Kingdom purpose. In my eyes, I still saw myself as the average kid from Battle Creek. Knowing what God thought of me, freed me from the bondage of an orphan spirit. I did not have to work to earn love that was already mine. There is nothing that would change me from loving my sons unconditionally, and I now know that is what my heavenly Father thinks of me.

The Next Step

Once I got that revelation from the Holy Spirit, I had to then feed my spirit with fasting and prayer. I had to make sure that I was connected to others that also know who they are in Christ. I had to stay connected to strong and bold individuals that knew their identity. When you are around others who are confident in who God called them to be and know who they are, an impartation happens. You will begin to walk in more boldness and courage, as you are positively influenced by their example.

In the beginning, all my connections were not personal connections. The Lord led me to invest in myself through books, webinars, and mentoring and coaching courses. I will give you more details later on in the book on these resources. But suffice to say, the information I received imparted a wealth on the inside of me. Did you catch that? He imparted wealth on the inside of me—He imparted wisdom to prosper in every area of my life.

When you have wisdom, you then have wealth. God wants to release wealth out of you, but not only in the form of money. Wealth is more than having financial influence; it is influence with people—the influence to have followers and those that serve you, and the influence to have strength in a battle.

Do you see why the enemy does not want you to know who you are? He wants to destroy your influence. You are assigned to some people, nations and generations;

you need to know who you are in Christ, and you need His wisdom. You are not qualified for wealth if you do not have wisdom.

God was showing us through King Solomon that we do not qualify for wealth unless we have wisdom. Wisdom is what King Solomon asked for over wealth, and because he had wisdom, he could steward material wealth. I encourage you to ask God to solidify your identity in Him and to grant you Wisdom in every area of your life.

> If any of you lacks wisdom,
> you should ask God,
> who gives generously to all without finding fault,
> and it will be given to you.
> James 1:5

My Steps to Overcoming Abandonment and Rejection

- **Deliverance**: I initially had no idea that I had abandonment issues until a deliverance session at my church during that time. My pastor was taking me through deliverance and calling out some other spirits that I was dealing with, such as anger, bitterness and rejection. If you know a little about the deliverance ministry, you know that some spirits can hide.

  Not only that, it is easier for the lower level demonic spirits to leave, and they usually leave first. I was going through deliverance, and the spirits operating in me began to get stubborn and were starting to resist the deliverance session. Through discernment and the Holy Spirit, it was revealed to my pastor that I had the spirit of abandonment from my father. I broke when he began to deal with the spirit of abandonment.

When that session was over, I was in total shock that I was dealing with that spirit, but it was evident through the deliverance that I was. The spirit of abandonment was hidden for so long that I was not aware of his presence. **Side note**: Some of you are going through deliverance in areas and afraid to seek spiritual counseling. In the process of deliverance and even after deliverance is complete, spiritual counseling and discipleship are needed to help you with maintaining your deliverance.

- **Healing**: When dealing with the spirit of abandonment, it is always necessary to go through the healing process. I went through deliverance, but now I needed to go through soul healing. I went to another deliverance ministry that also worked heavily in the healing ministry. Through the healing process, God allowed me to see His thoughts towards me. I had to exchange my thoughts of abandonment from my biological father, for thoughts about a loving Father that would never leave me nor forsake me. I came to understand that He didn't make a mistake when He made me, and that it was also necessary for me to have the parents that He chose for me.

- **Forgiveness**: Sometimes, we get so caught up in who our parents are and do not realize that it was for a purpose that God allowed your parents to be your parents. If you have not already, you must forgive your parent(s) for abandoning you. Most of the time, it has nothing to do with you at all. It is because of their own issues or inadequacies, or because of what they too went through growing up. Also, your mother or father may not have had a father in their life to teach them. Have mercy and grace on your parent(s). You have a heavenly Father that forgives and wants you to embrace the love that He has to offer you.

- **Trust in God, not man**: I had an impartation that came from a vision that I had of my Daddy (Jesus Christ). He was letting me know that He accepts me as His own—His daughter, and that I did not have to perform for Him or work to gain His love because I already had it. When I was able to see how He truly felt about me, I was no longer concerned about the others' viewpoint of me because they didn't create me, and neither is my destiny in their hands.

Here is a word of wisdom for you: Stop putting your destiny and purpose in other people's hands. No one can stop the plan and purposes that God has for your life. When you begin to believe that people have a responsibility for your future, and not God, you will begin to perform for those people. You will begin to work to gain their praise and approval because you are not putting your trust in God or believing in Him for your future. The problem is, you think that God has disqualified you and will count you out because of your mistakes that you may make during the process. You may also dismiss the prophetic words that have been spoken over your life because of your mistakes or for not being fully mature in your skills, talents, or gifts. However, it is God that brings the increase in your life; it is God that gives you a measure of faith to operate in the gifts of the Spirit, not man. So, trust in God, not man.

- **Stop comparing yourself!** When you compare yourself to others, you are ultimately not trusting God with the gift that He has given you; you in effect are saying, *"God I do not trust you to increase this gift in my life."* Do you think that the people you are comparing yourself to started out on top or mature in their gift or talents? Sometimes people get prideful or arrogant when they reach a certain level and forget where they came from, and look down on those that are just coming up or starting out. Sometimes, they feel threatened by you because they are using their gifts out of selfish ambition and they will try to discourage you. Keep your eyes focused on the prize—Jesus Christ! Do not let the spirit of intimidation cause you to draw back into forgetting that you are a daughter of the King! The Bible says in Hebrews 12:1-3 that we are to, "throw off everything that hinders and the sin that so easily entangles. And let us run with perseverance the race marked out for us, fixing our eyes on Jesus, the pioneer and perfecter of faith.

For the joy set before him he endured the cross, scorning its shame, and sat down at the right hand of the throne of God. Consider him who endured such opposition from sinners, so that you will not grow weary and lose heart.

- **Keep growing**: Read a book such as "Experiencing Father's Embrace" by Jack Frost to maintain your deliverance; and any other book that speaks on your relationship with Jesus Christ.

- **Feed on God's Word:** Don't forget to read the Word of God daily and to keep praying and depending on Jesus in all that you do. Ask Him to give you the strength to "do" His Word and not just "hear" it.

Remember what James 1: 22-25 says, "Do not merely listen to the word, and so deceive yourselves. Do what it says. Anyone who listens to the word but does not do what it says is like someone who looks at his face in a mirror and, after looking at himself, goes away and immediately forgets what he looks like. But whoever looks intently into the perfect law that gives freedom, and continues in it—not forgetting what they have heard, but doing it—they will be blessed in what they do."

My Prayer for You

Father God in the Name of Jesus, I pray that the woman of God that is reading this prayer will no longer be bound by the spirit of rejection or abandonment. I pray that she will forgive everyone that she has felt rejection or abandonment from. I speak freedom to her mind, will and emotions from every memory recall of those that have hurt her in the Name of Jesus. I pray that she will seek her affirmation and validation through You. I pray that she will know that her purpose rests in You, and You alone. Father God, I pray that You will reveal who she is through Your eyes and show her–her Kingdom assignment while on Earth. I pray that every deceiving spirit that will tell her that she is not worthy, or that she is alone, will be broken NOW, in the Name of Jesus! Lord, I thank you that her identity is in You! Rejection and abandonment are no longer keeping her bound. Lord, I thank you that she is no longer walking in anger, bitterness, unforgiveness, jealous, or strife. Lord, I thank you for breaking the spirit of pride that is rooted in rejection and abandonment. Lord, I thank you that she has the heart of the Father, and is not ruled by negative emotions. Thank you Lord for guarding her heart from deceptive spirits and spirits of error. Thank you, Jesus, for filling her heart with the heart of the Father. Thank you, Jesus, that she is not easily offended! I pray that the spirit of offense and oversensitivity will be broken NOW, in Jesus' Name! Thank you, Jesus, that you are restoring her original identity that You predestined before the foundation of the world! Lord, I thank you that she is not drawing back from You when she makes a mistake or rejected by others. I pray that the spirit of insecurity will be broken and that the spirit of trust and security in you will be loosed in her heart, mind and soul. Thank you, Jesus, for healing every deep wound of hurt from her childhood. Lord, I thank You that she has let go of the past and is moving forward towards the mark of the high calling in Christ Jesus! Thank you Jesus, that she is fearfully and wonderfully made, and has an expected in. She shall live and not die, and declare the works of the Lord. In Jesus' Name, Amen!

Chapter 15

The Helmet of Salvation and the Holy Spirit

The Helmet of Salvation: Guard Your Mind

Remember when I experienced the severe attack of depression a while after I surrendered to God and said, "Yes"? It reminds me of Job. Satan had permission to touch Job in any way—but he could not kill him. It was as if Satan had permission to attack me severely, but he could not kill me. The first thing the enemy attacked was my mind. He wanted to drive me crazy, to the point where I would give up in the very area that I was giving birth to— another level of intercession and warfare.

The enemy will attack your mind first to get you off course. The mind determines the course of our lives. Therefore, God tells us to put on the helmet of salvation. Ephesians 6:17 says, "Take the helmet of salvation and the sword of the Spirit, which is the word of God." A part of our spiritual armor is the helmet of salvation.

Back in Apostle Paul's time, the helmet was put on as a protector for the head, face and back of neck. If there was a blow to the head, the rest of the armor would be of little to no use. One terrible blow to the head could possibly cause brain injury. If brain injury occurs, you could lose your speech, become paralyzed and experience memory loss. The brain controls the rest of the body's function. Even several hits to the head can potentially be danger-ous and can cause internal bleeding and wounds. You are of no use to fight in the battle if you have had an injury to your head; it would be too hard to fight and it will make you vulnerable to a quicker death, so you would need to depend on your battle buddy to fight for you.

Now that is some revelation knowledge right there... We are to carry each other's burdens when one is too weak to pray or fight on their own, or in a battle that is too strong to fight. Galatians 6:2 states, "Carry each other's burdens, and in this way, you will fulfill the law of Christ." When I was overtaken by depression and the attack was so strong, I called on my battle buddies (intercessors and prayer partners) to stand in the gap until I gained enough faith and strength to pray and war for myself. I do not like it when I hear people of God say, "When you are going through something, you need to pray and lay hands on yourself instead of calling someone." Yes, we need to be able to pray for ourselves, but it is unbiblical to say that we do not need someone to pray for us or stand in the gap when we are weak or under a strong attack. The Bible does talk about us being the body of Christ, and we need each other to function and to carry each other's burdens.

Back to the helmet of salvation; the enemy is after your salvation. He is out to kill, steal and destroy. If he can steal your salvation, then he has stolen your soul. The helmet of salvation is your security in Jesus Christ—it is your confidence in who you are in Christ. Salvation is your security deposit that you are in right standing with Jesus Christ. Salvation is your joy and peace that carries you through the battle. Did you catch that revelation? If not, let me break it down for you.

As I stated previously, in the natural, if you get blows to the head or one had a hard hit to the head, you can become severely paralyzed, suffer memory loss, lose your speech and potentially die. Keeping the head protected is important in winning and fighting a battle. Therefore, in the spiritual, having on the helmet of salvation guarantees you peace (that the world cannot give) and joy. We need peace and joy to carry us through the storms, tests and tribulations.

When we have our helmet of salvation on, our peace and joy is intact. The helmet of salvation causes us to be content. If the enemy can strip you of your peace, then he has an open door and access to torment your mind. Be free in your mind and think on things that are above; things that are of good report. Take the time to think and ponder on who God says you are; what God says your purpose is. If you do not know, pray and ask God to show you.

Phil 4:8, "Finally, brothers and sisters, whatever is true, whatever is noble, whatever is right, whatever is pure, whatever is lovely, whatever is admirable—if anything is excellent or praiseworthy—think about such things."

The Holy Spirit—Trust in Him

During my attack of depression, it was only through God's grace that was working through the Holy Spirit that gave me the strength to endure. Without the presence and promptings of the Holy Spirit, I would have not made it. As I have mentioned before, one of the many benefits of being saved is the indwelling of the Holy Spirit. The Holy Spirit has so many functions, and one of them is to grant strength—the ability to do the right thing when you are faced with temptations.

It was the Holy Spirit that prompted me to call on others to pray for me. It was the prompting of the Holy Spirit that led me to read the book of Psalms and it was the prompting of the Holy Spirit that directed me to the doctor's office. It was the prompting of the Holy Spirit that told me to, "Get up—put on some clothes, put your make-up on, and go to the mall." I had to force myself to listen to His voice. I believed the Word of the Lord and was desperate to get out of my situation. When I got up and went to the mall, I ended up getting a massage while I was there. I felt so much better for doing what the Holy Spirit prompted me to do. He knew what I needed to strengthen me to press forward. It reminded me of when the angel of the Lord told Elijah to get up and eat.

The Holy Spirit taught me perseverance during this attack, and the perseverance developed my character. Romans 5:4, "Not only so, but we also glory in our sufferings, because we know that suffering produces perseverance; perseverance, character; and character, hope. And hope does not put us to shame, because God's love has been poured out into our hearts through the Holy Spirit, who has been given to us." Our flesh wants to give up in the battle because of the pain that we are enduring. No one really likes to go through pain. At least, I don't, but the pain that comes from trials, tribulations and attacks is actually building your character and spiritual muscles. There is no other way to build spiritual muscles but through some type of hardship, it's easy to stay standing when everything is going well—but your faith is tested when all hell breaks loose.

There are so many people that die in their present situation because they do not have the Holy Spirit, and some people have the Holy Spirit but don't listen to what He is telling them to do. If you have the Holy Spirit living on the inside of you, listen to His promptings and listen to His instructions, even when it seems ridiculous. At the time, I wanted to lie down and die to escape the pressure of depression, but the Holy Spirit told me to "Get up." I did not think I had enough strength to get up, but God knew that if I obeyed Him, He would carry me and He was faithful to strengthen me.

I've spoken in depth about my experience with depression in Chapter 8. These are a few of the steps that I followed to become set free from depression.

My Steps to Being Set Free from Depression

- During the time that I was throwing up every morning, God told me that He was getting some things out of me that I did not know was there. God Himself was taking me through deliverance. All the weight I lost was symbolic or prophetic of everything I was getting rid of. At the time, I needed physical intervention until my spiritual breakthrough came forth. If you are going through a similar process, you may need physical intervention to sustain your body. Try to get sufficient sleep and eat a healthy diet. If you are prompted to see a doctor, follow the Holy Spirit's leading. I needed help with medication until the spiritual breakthrough came forth.

Side note: Some of you are going through deliverance in different areas and afraid to seek spiritual counseling. In the process of deliverance, and even after deliverance is complete, spiritual counseling and discipleship are needed to help you with maintaining your deliverance. Don't be afraid to seek help. You will need the support.

- The battle was too strong for me so I had to reach out to other intercessors and prayer warriors that I "KNOW" pray. It is important for you to let your pride, guilt and shame down and reach out to others that will pray and stand in the gap for you. I cannot stress letting your pride down and reaching out to trusted individuals to pray and encourage you. Individuals that are in leadership positions, or the strong ones often have a hard time reaching out for help because they are the ones that are always giving help, or have the appearance of always having it together. This is far from the truth. Your life can literally depend on you getting help.

We have all been through some type of storm, and it takes others to help pull us out of some storms.

- There were moments that I could not pray for myself because I was so depressed, and crying out to God to deliver me. Depression is a spirit from the devil; therefore, you must engage the enemy with Scriptures. I could not pray for myself at times, but I was able to read the Book of Psalms. Read passages and chapters in the Book of Psalms out loud that deal with engaging the enemy. Remember, you are not fighting against the flesh and blood but rulers, authorities, powers and spiritual forces of evil. Ephesians 6:12, "For our struggle is not against flesh and blood, but against the rulers, against the authorities, against the powers of this dark world, and against the spiritual forces of evil in the heavenly realms."

- I read warfare prayers every day on a consistent basis because I knew I was in a spiritual battle. Do not let up on these prayers until you KNOW that you have complete victory. Sometimes, people stop reading prayers or warfare prayers too soon, without having the manifestation of a complete victory.

- I listened to worship music day in and day out. One of my favorites was "You are my Peace" by Juanita Bynum. I had no peace and wanted that song to rest in my spirit and drive the spirit of depression away. Saul had an evil spirit and wanted King David to play the harp to drive the evil spirit away. 1 Samuel 16:23, "Whenever the spirit from God came on Saul, David would take up his lyre and play. Then relief would come to Saul; he would feel better, and the evil spirit would leave him." Worship! Worship! Worship!

- Spiritual attacks also take a toll on your physical body. During my depression, I was not eating; therefore, I was not getting the nutrients that I needed. Take vitamins and natural supplements that will aid your sleeping and feeling more relaxed.

  I was advised by a nutritionist to take serotonin and essential amino acids to aid my mood, to feel more relaxed and assist with sleeping. Reach out to a nutritionist or holistic advisor on the best supplements to take during this time.

- Go get a massage. A massage helps relax your muscles and relieves stress.

- Force yourself to get up and get out! You must press your way through this—but you can do it. Comb your hair, put on your make-up if you wear make-up, and get dressed. Go do something that you like to do.

- Make sure you stay connected to your church home, and don't be prideful to go to the altar to get some prayer. If you have to lay out on the altar and cry out to God, then by all means, lay out. There is no time for you to be worried or concerned about your image or ego. The fresh anointing that will be placed on your life when you come out is well worth it.

- During my time of depression, my church was not yet operating in the deliverance ministry, and I was just learning about deliverance. Go get some deliverance!

- During my time of depression, the Holy Spirit was also taking me through supernatural deliverance and teaching me to war. What the devil meant for bad turned out to be a birthing of something new.

The anointing will cost you something. Seek God on what He is birthing out of you through this process. The crushing hurts, but it is worth it!

My Prayer for You

Father God in the Name of Jesus, I pray that depression will be broken off the woman of God reading this. I pray that every seed of depression that would try to take root will be broken NOW, in the Name of Jesus! I pray that depression will leave her emotions and that she will be healed from deep hurt. I pray that every spirit of heaviness will be broken, and that you will give her garments of praise and joy. Father God, restore the joy of her salvation; restore her peace O God. I pray that she will walk in forgiveness for herself and will not be bound by the spirit of condemnation. Lord, I thank you for breaking every tormenting spirit that would torment her mind, body and soul. Thank you Lord that you are granting her rest and peaceful sleep. Father, I pray that you will connect her with other intercessors and prayer warriors that will speak life into her and pray on her behalf. Thank you, Jesus, for giving her the strength to press pass this trail. I pray that the spirit of suicide will be broken off of her mind, and every thought of suicide will be broken NOW in Jesus' Name! I pray that every thought to give up will be filled with hope. In the Name of Jesus, I pray that every demonic time-released assignment that is coming against her life be broken! Thank you, Jesus, that you are releasing a fresh anointing and power upon her. Thank you, Jesus, that you are bringing her to a new level of intercession and pursuit for you. Lord, I thank you that she is receiving new revelations from you that are speaking life into her spirit. Thank you, Lord, for releasing ministering angels and angels of comfort in this time and season to carry her. Thank you, Jesus, that fear no longer has its grip, and You are uplifting her with your mighty Hand. In Jesus' Name, Amen!

Chapter 16

The Deliverance

What is deliverance for those that may ask? Deliverance in a nutshell is freedom from demonic or evil spirits. There can be evil spirits of rejection, abandonment, poverty, depression, addiction, gluttony, witchcraft, anger, unforgiveness, bitterness, confusion; the list can go on and on. There can be demonic strongholds over your life that have caused your freedom of choice to be taken away from you. Have you repented and asked God for forgiveness, but found yourself back doing the same cycle over and over? If this is the case, then you are most likely under a demonic stronghold or evil spirits are influencing your behavior.

Now, there are works of the flesh (the sin nature) which can be found in Galatians 5:19-21, "The acts of the flesh are obvious: sexual immorality, impurity and debauchery; idolatry and witchcraft; hatred, discord, jealousy, fits of rage, selfish ambition, dissensions, factions and envy; drunkenness, orgies, and the like. I warn you, as I did before, that those who live like this will not inherit the kingdom of God." When you are a born-again believer, you should ask for forgiveness, repent and turn from that particular sin, but again, if you find yourself repeating the same thing after much prayer and repentance, it's time for deliverance.

In this book, I have named several evil strongholds that were operating in my life which were rejection, abandonment, depression, perfectionism, resentment and anger, and I thank God for His deliverance. I didn't know that

I was under demonic influence and stronghold. I didn't even identify myself with some of these issues, except for the obvious ones such as anger.

As I drew closer to God, He revealed to me through Dr. Cindy Trimm's book, *Rules of Engagement* that I had strongholds in my life. I didn't even know what spiritual warfare was, until I read her book. I learned that there are many other evil spirits attached to one, which is called the root. The root is what is causing the other spirits to operate in your life. For example, a spirit of rejection can bring bitterness, resentment, people-pleasing, spirit of offense, oversensitivity, jealousy, strife, anger, deep wounds of hurt, pride, fear, lack of trust, and several other spirits. I was first opened to all of this while reading Dr. Cindy Trimm's book; I spoken prayers that I had never prayed before. Once I became knowledgeable of evil spirits and demons, I naturally did not want to be influenced by them. I was faithful in reading warfare prayers. I am not going to go in depth regarding deliverance in this book. There are many resources and authors out there that cover deliverance such as John Eckhardt's book *Deliverance and Spiritual Warfare Manual*, *Pigs in the Parlor* by Frank Hammond and Ida Mae Hammond; and Derek Prince has teachings on YouTube.

The Deliverance Process

The first step in being delivered started with becoming aware that I had evil spirits operating in and influencing me. When I realized that I was indeed being influenced by demons, I also realized that I needed a Savior to save me from those demonic influences.

Let me stop right here for a minute: A believing Christian of Jesus Christ cannot be demon possessed but *influenced* by a demon. Believers belong to Jesus, and not owned by the devil.

When I recognized that I needed help, I confessed my sins unto God and asked His forgiveness. He is faithful and just to forgive us, and cleanse us from all unrighteousness when we come to Him with a sincere and pure heart. I acknowledged my sin; confessed my sin and then renounced my sin.

By verbally renouncing the sin that is operating in your life, you are telling the devil that you come out of agreement with him, and that you are no longer giving him legal grounds to stay present in your life.

A deliverance minister can walk you through this process, and you can also walk yourself through this process. However, there are times when you need someone's authority to cast the demon or evil spirits out of you. Once you confess, repent and renounce, now it's time for the evil spirit to be cast out of you. This is done with authority. Demons only recognize authority. Demons expel themselves through the power and authority that the person, or yourself, carries through the power of Jesus Christ. The demonic spirits expel through coughing, sneezing, crying, passing gas, bowel movements, vomiting or screaming. They come in through an opening and they must leave through an opening.

Maintaining Your Deliverance

Many people tend to think this, "I've been through all of the formalities of deliverance; now I am FREE! I am good and can go on my merry way." But that is not the case. Deliverance is not a magic pill or potion that "fixes" the problem. Deliverance is the first step, now comes maintaining your deliverance.

Jesus says the following in Luke 11:24-26, "When an impure spirit comes out of a person, it goes through arid places seeking rest and does not find it. Then it says, 'I will return to the house I left.' When it arrives, it finds the house swept clean and put in order. Then it goes and takes seven other spirits more wicked than itself, and they go in and live there. And the final condition of that person is worse than the first."

If you do not have a prayer life, or a life of reading the Word of God to "fill your house" then those demons will come back very easily. You also need to make sure you are watching what you put into your spirit and where you go. If you have just been delivered from being addicted to drugs, and think you are straight and strong enough to put yourself back in those same environments around those same people—you have definitely mistaken deliverance. Jesus gives us wisdom, and we are to cling to what is good and avoid evil. It doesn't make sense to run towards temptation; that makes no sense at all. You have to know the weaknesses and the triggers in your flesh that will draw you back to those things.

Please do not open yourself up to be tempted to do the very thing that you were delivered from. There has to be some disconnections from relationships and environments in order to maintain your deliverance. However, whenever you remove something, you need to replace it with something else. The same goes for friendships and environments. Surround yourself with people and places that will encourage you to maintain your deliverance.

Discipleship is vital after deliverance. You need to gain knowledge into the Scriptures and be rooted and grounded in the Word. Once the Word is rooted and grounded in you, and you have an intimacy with the Holy Spirit and are filled with the Holy Spirit and Fire; it will not be easy for you to be tempted by things. I was delivered from smoking marijuana a very long time ago. I can no longer be tempted in that area. If I smell weed, I am not tempted to want to go smoke. I learned early on that if I am still having troubles in an area of weakness, to not run to or be around the very person or situation that I am weak in. When you don't recognize your weaknesses, then you can be your worst enemy. That's where discipleship and accountability comes in. Surround yourself with other women of God and don't allow the spirit of fear or doubt stagnate you from moving into your purpose.

My Steps to Deliverance

- Worship: It is always good to start out with worship before you take yourself through deliverance.

- Forgive: Ask the Holy Spirit if there is anyone in your heart that you need to forgive. Begin to decide to forgive and let go immediately! When you forgive others, your Heavenly Father will forgive you!

- Plead the Blood of Jesus over yourself and loose warring angels in the atmosphere.

- There are some sins and behaviors that are generational. The Holy Spirit will also reveal to you if the sins and behaviors that you are carrying are from your parents, or your parent's parents or ancestors. If what is in your soul is from your ancestors, ask God to forgive them for that sin and renounce those things.

- Here is a sample prayer that you could pray:

Dear Heavenly Father, in the Name of Jesus, I confess that I am angry (the Holy Spirit will reveal to you the sin and even the cause of it). I ask that you forgive me of anger. I repent before you now. I renounce the spirit of anger and every fruit that is rooted in anger (the Holy Spirit will reveal to you other spirits that are associated with anger, that you need deliverance from). I renounce the spirit of anger, and thank you Jesus for cleansing me of all unrighteousness. I speak to the spirit of anger and command it to come out now, in the name of Jesus! I break the spirit of anger out of my mind, will and emotions in the name of Jesus!

- Ask Jesus to remove the effects of trauma that occurred in your life and to even remove the memories of those traumas. The enemy likes to bring memories to mind that recall the hurt and pain from those that wrongfully used you.

- Submit to the Holy Spirit and allow whatever spirit you are calling out to be expelled. Do not allow pride to interfere with your deliverance. There are areas that the Holy Spirit will reveal to you that you need deliverance from, and you may not have known you had those evil spirits operating in your life because there are times when evil spirits hide or lay dormant for many years. Yield to the Holy Spirit and allow Him to do the work. Do not be dismayed if you did not know that these evil spirits are in the inside of you.

- Confess, ask for forgiveness, repent, renounce, and be free.

- Ask the Holy Spirit to reveal the root. Evil spirits are just like seeds; they grow over time if they were never cast out or dealt with. Destroy the root and the branches will die.

- Deliverance is not a once and for all ordeal; we will go through deliverance for the entire time that we are in these bodies. It is a process to be whole in every area of your life. Don't despise the process and forward march into your destiny.

My Prayer for You

Dear Heavenly Father, I thank you that the woman of God reading this prayer is walking in the manifestation of her deliverance. If she has not received deliverance, I pray that you will cause her to encounter deliverance from every stronghold that is over her life. Lord, I thank you that she is being discipled and learning from your Word. I thank you Lord that she is faithful to You. Thank you, Lord, that she is walking in obedience and resisting the devil. Thank you, Jesus, that she is finding a way of escape from every temptation. Lord I thank you that she will always be hungry and thirsty for your Word. I thank you that she is a doer of Your word, and not just a hearer. Thank you, Jesus, that she is rightly dividing the Word of Truth! Thank you, Jesus, that she delights in your Word and mediates on Your Word day and night! Thank you, Jesus, that she is quick to repent and You are faithful to forgive her from all unrighteousness. Thank you Lord that Your Word is hidden in her heart that she may not sin against You. Thank you, Lord that she is filled with the Holy Spirit and Fire. Lord, I thank you that she can pray with Fire, minister with Fire and prophesy with Fire. Thank you Lord that she is following the leading and promptings of the Holy Spirit; she is walking in the spirit and not the flesh. Thank you Lord that she is walking in the fruit of the Spirit, and that you are increasing her daily. Lord, I thank you that Your Glory is shining through her! In Jesus' Name, Amen!

.

Chapter 17

The Seeds

The seed that Jesus Christ plants in our hearts never dies while we are here on Earth. It does not matter if that seed was planted in you as a child, a teenager or an adult. It doesn't matter if you grew up in the things of God and fell away, or if you believed in the gospel of Jesus Christ but did not surrender fully. The seed of Jesus Christ is still in you. "The Word became flesh and made his dwelling among us. We have seen his glory, the glory of the one and only Son, who came from the Father, full of grace and truth." John 1:14

The other day, I was thinking about seeds, and I googled the life span of a seed that has been planted in the ground. I found some interesting facts:

Seeds can remain dormant for weeks or even years before they produce. I also found out that there was a scientist by the name of William James Beal who started a 100-year long experiment. He put seeds into 20 time capsules and dug one up every 5 years. The experiment is still going on today and the researchers who are carrying on his work, have found that some of the twenty-five-year-old seeds can still sprout. It has also been noted by a scientist by the name of Jane Shen-Miller that the oldest living seed to germinate is over 1000 years old.

Remember the seed that God has put in you stays planted in your heart while you are here on earth. When you accept Jesus Christ in your life as your Lord and personal Savior, God plants an eternal seed into your heart.

God first loved us—we did not first love Him, and He chose us while we were lost, so once His seed is planted in you, there is nothing that can uproot it because it is His desire that no one perishes but that all come under repentance and have eternal life. 2 Peter 3:9, "The Lord is not slow in keeping his promise, as some understand slowness. Instead he is patient with you, not wanting anyone to perish, but everyone to come to repentance."

The seed will remain dormant waiting to produce. God will bring others your way to water the seed that is already on the inside of you, through prayer, encouraging words, prophecies, sermons, gospel songs, books, and even godly movies. He is watching over the Word and waiting patiently. Isaiah 27:2-3, "In that day "Sing about a fruitful vineyard: I, the Lord, watch over it; I water it continually. I guard it day and night so that no one may harm it."

The seed that grows will not bear fruit in your life until you are fully connected to Him. The fruit that God wants to bring forth in your life is love, joy, peace, forbearance, kindness, goodness, faithfulness, gentleness and self-control. When we are not connected to the Vine (Jesus Christ), we can bear nothing. John 15:5, "I am the vine; you are the branches. If you remain in me and I in you, you will bear much fruit; apart from me you can do nothing."

Jesus Christ is our Chief Intercessor that is praying on your behalf, to God, day and night, along with the other saints. Therefore, it is so important for the people of God to be praying on a daily basis for the lost sheep and the seeds of Abraham. We are to be praying continually for their souls to be saved, and for them to come into the knowledge of Jesus Christ. He has called us and them from the foundation of the world—and He is waiting on a surrendered and committed yes.

Once you say "yes", He is going to bring forth the love of the Father into your heart. He is going to put the Holy Spirit on the inside of you to bring forth Truth—to be your Comforter, Advocate and Strength. He is going to give you a peace and joy that the world cannot give. He is going to lavish you with His goodness. There will be tests, trials and tribulations, I am not going to sit here and lie to you and say that it is going to always be easy or a bowl of ice cream, but you will have the security, love and protection of a Father to be right there with you through it ALL! He is your great DELIVERER!

Seeds of Darkness

The enemy can also plant seeds, but when he plants a seed of abandonment, rejection, anger, pride, bitterness, unforgiveness, etc., it begins to flourish and spread quickly like a cancer. One seed can bring forth an increase of more spirits operating in your life and they remain until they are uprooted and cast out.

There are some spirits that will leave by the mere presence of God being active in your life, and the light and love of Jesus Christ that has entered in. Where there is light, darkness is exposed and cast out. But just like how a natural seed can remain dormant for years, so can a demonic seed that is not dealt with. The enemy will continue to bring people and situations in your life to water that seed of abandonment and rejection that was planted early on.

It is a constant war for your soul. God brings people and situations in your life to water the seed of the Word; and the enemy brings people and situations to water the seed of abandonment and rejection. Ask the Holy Spirit to reveal the "weeds" that are growing and operating in your life. Unless He reveals it, we don't see them; and the enemy of our souls and our flesh nature continues to water them.

Which seeds are you going to water? Are you watering the seeds of darkness or faith? Which ones are you going to uproot and pull out, and which one are you going to nurture?

Children and Seeds of Faith

I know it is hard to believe that I did all of those things: drinking, marijuana and sex, at such a young age. But nowadays, I know it isn't a surprise what our young people are doing. Well, my testimony shows that it is nothing new.

A lot of times, people are quick to blame the parent(s) for the choices their children make, and don't get me wrong; there are times when it is the parent(s) fault, but not always. A parent can do everything that they know to do to raise their children the right way and protect them—and the child still goes in a total opposite direction. That child was me. We were not a Cosby Show family growing up but we were brought up with morals, values, and my mom kept us in church. However, as humans, we are born in our iniquities (sin). No one has to teach us how to sin; we are in it. Our very first nature is to sin until God chooses us out of darkness, and puts us into His marvelous light.

The enemy's agenda is to water the seed of sin and kill our purpose and destiny before we get to it. There is a certain age. Usually when they hit their teenage years, that children begin to have their own mind and want to do what they want to do, no matter what. No matter how much you discipline them, sometimes they are still rebellious and disobedient. I was that teenager; I did not care how much I was disciplined or put on punishment. The sin of rebellion was rooted in me strongly, and no discipline from my mother or stepfather would stop me. I had an agenda and that agenda was going to be fulfilled by any means necessary.

Don't you know that is the same tactic of the enemy? The devil wants to fulfill his agenda by any means necessary. If you are a parent out there, do not be discouraged. Keep praying, fasting, warring and believing for your children. Those seeds that you planted in them as children, will bear fruit in due season. I am a living witness.

My Steps to Sowing Seeds of Faith

- The Seeds of Faith comes by staying connected to the Vine, which is Jesus Christ and believing what the Word of God says.

- Consistently deposit what is good in your eyes and ears. Reject negativity when you recognize it; it is trying to influence your emotions and conduct.

- The more good that you deposit in your life, the stronger your faith becomes. Defeat fear by moving in boldness and courage in who God called you to be.

- Sowing seeds of faith is to not believe the lies of the enemy that you will always go through rejection, abandonment, anger, depression or whatever it is.

- Repeat after me – "I believe who God says I am; and I am free from (fill in the blank), even though I don't see it."

My Prayer for You

Lord, I thank you for the good seeds that your daughter is planting in her heart. Thank you for uprooting the bad seeds of anger, bitterness, depression, unforgiveness, rejection, abandonment, pride and hurt from her heart. Thank you Lord for removing the thorns and thistles that choke up the bad seeds. I thank you Lord that her heart is the heart of flesh, and she is able to receive your Word, and the wisdom that comes from your Word. I thank you Lord that she is sowing seeds of righteousness and reaping a harvest of love. Thank you Lord that she is sowing in peace and reaping a harvest of righteousness. Thank you Lord that she is connected to You, the Vine, and bearing much fruit. Thank you Lord that she is reaping some thirty, sixty and one-hundred-fold return for the good she has sown. She has given love and now reaping an abundance of love; she has shown mercy and now reaping an abundance of mercy; she has shown kindness and now reaping an abundance of kindness. Thank you Lord that your daughter is entering into her fruitful place and bringing forth much increase in every area of her life: spiritually, physically, emotionally, and financially. In Jesus' Name, Amen!

Chapter 18

Relationships and Ungodly Soul Ties

True Identity and Relationships

Love is so superficial when you are a young teenager. When you are that young, "love" is based on mere appearance and attraction, and you really think that you are going to be with that person forever.

When I was fourteen to fifteen years old, I used to sneak my boyfriend into the house quite a bit. We were not having sex; I was still a virgin, but what we did was lay down, hugged up on the couch, French kissing—as if we were married. At that moment, when I was hugged up and exchanging saliva with my boyfriend, I thought we were going to be together forever. I remember him giving me a school picture of himself and on the back, it said, "I will always love you forever." At that age, you are quick to say, "I love you" based on, "he is so cute and she is so fine."

However, the enemy begins to establish soul ties and opens more doors of perversion at that young age. His agenda is to get you early, so that the seed of perversion can begin to take root and manifest its fruit through demonic soul ties, wrong connections, the wrong identity, fornication, adultery, masturbation and even mental illness. There is a hidden spiritual truth that the enemy does not want you to know—he uses the things that God has called blessed, and perverts it for his agenda.

Sex and tongue kissing is not bad in itself; they are gifts from God for you and your husband. When you do this out of wedlock, you are entering a level of intimacy that opens the door for a demonic soul tie. Yes, this can happen through exchanging saliva and having sex. A connection with the wrong person, out of the marriage covenant, can create a demonic soul tie. A negative, demonic soul tie is when there is a linkage of two souls that brings forth negative results and manifestations.

Demonic and negative soul ties will cause you to operate in rebellion; you will begin to do things for the sake of that person or persons. Emotional soul ties will blind you to not think about the consequences of your actions. The person begins to be your idol because you have now set your affections on nothing but that individual. The Word of God says for us to put no other gods before Him. When we put all our affections onto an ungodly relationship, it is idolatry. Anything that you put before Him is idolatry. The devil wants to set idolatry in your heart and soul at a young age. He wants to put the root of rebellion in your heart, and what better way but to open up the door of perversion and lust. A soul connection with the wrong person defiles and corrupts your soul, and transfers demonic spirits into your soul.

Let's discuss demonic spirits being transferred into your soul for a minute. I Corinthians 6:16, "Do you know that he who unites himself with a prostitute is one with her in body? For it is said, 'The two will become one flesh.'" When you decide to have sex with someone other than the God ordained husband that God has for you, you become one with that person. Your soul becomes one with their soul, which means you lose your identity in who God created you to be before the foundation of the world. Ponder on that for a minute. Your identity is lost when you have sex with someone other than your spouse.

When a person has lost their identity, they lose the capacity to make the right decisions; they are influenced by the demonic and the ungodly soul ties. Even their appearance becomes distorted, meaning they will wear clothes or hairstyles that they normally would not wear, their words and language becomes corrupted, their emotions are unstable, and the demonic spirits that were already present, are magnified.

When you are being influenced by the demonic and controlled by the ungodly soul tie, undiagnosed mental illness can begin to manifest in your life, and most of the time you don't even realize it. At times, you may wonder why you feel like you are going crazy; or have an interest in doing things that you normally would not do—you can't think straight. You battle with your moods. You feel depressed; one minute you are up and then the next minute you are down; moody; an emotional roller coaster; a completely unstable person.

Remember, a soul tie can also come from connecting with ungodly relationships in a way that God has not ordained, and can have the same effect on your soul. The Bible states that evil company corrupts good manners. I Corinthians 15:33, "Do not be misled: 'Bad company corrupts good character.'" Parts of your soul becomes scattered among all of the people that you have made ungodly connections with, and you partake in the issues of their souls too. You can be negatively influenced by the ungodly connections, and you can lose your true identity even further.

Another way that the enemy operates is that the demonic recognizes the demonic. Have you ever wondered why you keep attracting the same type of person? Well, the demonic spirits in the soul of the person that you have become one with, transfer across to you, and the demons that are operating in the next person can recognize the similar spirits that are operating in you. Fruit is produced after its kind, and the agenda of the enemy is to keep producing his own kind—and multiplying it in you.

His agenda is to get you in deep by causing the demonic spirits that are operating in your life to become stronger and manifest on a greater level.

The loss of your true identity and the multiple soul ties will cause you to lose your vision and sense of self-worth. There needs to be deliverance from those soul ties, the demonic and a return of your true identity.

Connecting with Your True Identity and Purpose

Once you have accepted Jesus Christ into your life, the journey of healing and deliverance from the demonic and ungodly soul ties begins. When the people and the environment around you cause you to feel as if something is wrong with you because you are pursuing your spiritual and natural goals, then it is time for you to change environments and influences.

The real you cannot be birthed when you are around the wrong environment and people. The wrong environment and people will stagnate and sabotage your growth, and highest potential in Jesus Christ. It will distract you from your journey. For me, greatness was something that I kept feeling on the inside of me, but it was only a feeling because I didn't want to let go of my lifestyle, environment or friendships. Moving forward and advancing will cause you to leave some things behind, and this can be a challenge because who wants to leave behind that place of comfort; especially, genuine friendships that you love, and are most of the time like family? But God will bring you to a time and point in your life that you will no longer allow rejection to hold you back and you will find the courage to move on.

Once I connected with the right man, who is now my husband. I was able to connect to the right purpose and vision for my life. Our vision is one and lines up together; there is no confusion as to the vision that God has over our lives together.

If you are constantly in wrong, ungodly relationships, you are delaying your progress. We often pray and ask God to restore the years, but sometimes we need years restored because of the decisions we made in the past. I was in many wrong relationships in my time, but when I connected to the right husband; the years of my life began to be restored.

When the ungodly soul ties are broken and the negative influences removed, you will be able to identify your true self with your purpose. Your purpose will begin to manifest and everything that you once had a passion for, will come to the forefront.

I challenge you to disconnect from any ungodly relationships that God has not ordained to be a part of your life; your purpose depends on it. Don't allow yourself to be controlled by them like a puppet on a string. Make divine connections, and you will connect to your purpose!

My Steps to Breaking Ungodly Soul Ties

- I first had to recognize my self-worth; I had to recognize that I was deserving of better. You too Woman of God will have to recognize that you are deserving of better.

- Once I recognized my self-worth, I had to establish what was important to me and reevaluate the superficial things that I was paying attention too. Having a God-fearing husband and relationships that are godly in general are very important to me. Ask yourself,

'What type of relationship do I deserve to have in my life?' And make sure you are doing a soul check too.

- I had to forgive those that hurt me; with the help of God. It's okay to ask God for help in your areas of weakness, including unforgiveness.

- I had to go on continuous praying and fasting, and asking God to cleanse and purge me. We have not because we ask not. It is God's will for you to have a healthy soul!

- Trust God and His timing for the right relationships. When your soul is healed; it will make a difference in your life as a whole! I am a witness!

- An unhealthy soul will sabotage the right relationships that come in your life.

My Prayer for You

Thank you, Jesus, that you are breaking every ungodly soul tie NOW, in the Name of Jesus! Thank you, Jesus, for breaking every physical and emotional soul tie off of her life. Thank you, Jesus, for restoring her identity that has been lost in ungodly sexual soul ties. Lord, I thank you that you are bringing back to her the parts of her soul that have been fragmented and given to those that she has connected with out of Your will. I thank you Lord that she is identifying with her purpose and moving forward in her purpose and God-given gifts and talents. I thank you Lord that you are breaking low self-esteem and low self-worth NOW, in the Name of Jesus! I thank You Lord that her soul is being healed from any and all ill-spoken words that have been spoken over her life. I thank you Lord that she is precious in Your sight, and that You have called her queen; the apple of Your eye. Thank you Lord that there is no more delay upon her life because she trusts in who You say she is. I thank you for the Woman of God reading this prayer; and I thank you that she is fearfully and wonderfully made and set apart unto You. In Jesus' Name, Amen!

Chapter 19

How Clear is Your Vision?

Your eyes are an important part of TransHERmation. As people, we are drawn by what we see. I am a person that loves beautiful things and people. I am naturally inspired by beauty, and I love to decorate my home—that's my thing. Don't get me wrong. Like most ladies, I also enjoy buying shoes, clothes, jewelry, make-up and costume jewelry—I am drawn to beautiful costume jewelry.

I remember walking through an airport one day, and I saw this stand with beautiful dazzling jewelry; that jewelry caused me to turn my head all the way around. I lost my balance and fell, all because I was gazing at that beautiful necklace. I had to laugh at myself. I lost focus just that fast, and failed to focus on what was in front of me. When you are distracted, you are unable to see or focus on what is in front of you. Your eyes become fixed on something else and you can stumble and fall. What if I had hurt myself when I fell? It would have slowed me down in getting to my destination. This is what happens in the spiritual realm too. When you fix your eyes on something other than what God has for you, or begin to look back, it can cause you to be slowed down or to stagnate and remain in a place of complacency. God does not desire His daughters to be complacent.

He wants us to gaze upon His glory; His beauty. Did you know that one reference to glory is beauty? God wants to transform you into His glory; His beauty. He wants to manifest it through your smile, your song, your dance, your clothes, your home, your career, through every aspect of your life.

He wants to display His beauty. Do not be drawn back from God's glory because of what other people think of you or their own insecurities, I know I've mentioned it a few times, but it's so important—be free in being who God created you to be. God created you in His image and He wants to display His beauty through you. Think about this for a minute...God emptied Himself and made Himself of no reputation so that we can be rich through Him, which tells me that everything that radiates from God is beautiful, even the way heaven is described is beautiful... streets of gold and gates of pearls. Revelation 21:21, "The twelve gates were twelve pearls, each gate made of a single pearl. The great street of the city was of gold, as pure as transparent glass." I am not putting a focus on material possessions or even saying make your focus on material possessions, I am merely saying that when you obey God and keep Him first in your life, you do not have to be apologetic for how He rewards you with the manifestation of beauty; displaying the fruit of the Spirit in your life, and walking in love towards others.

Be confident in who you are in Christ; you do not have to prove yourself to anyone. Jesus knew who He was; and did not have to come to the Earth in a mink coat, Mercedes Benz or diamond rings. Jesus rode on a donkey—what God rode in did not determine His authority. He rode on a donkey and still turned water to wine, He still multiplied two fish and five loaves of bread and fed five thousand people. The authority He carried on earth spoke much more than earthly possessions.

The Pharisees...religious folks of those days, expected to see something different. They could not believe a carpenter such as Jesus, who they knew as Mary and Joseph's son, could possess so much authority. Girlfriend, they talked about Jesus—who holds all authority, so they will definitely talk about you. You may be judged or sized up because of your outward appearance, but they don't know you are a hidden treasure; a masterpiece; an under-cover jewel.

You will often be judged based on your current situation and circumstances. People will see you at your low state and whisper, gossip, and even speak ill of you, based on what their natural eyes see. Do not allow people to count you out because when God is for you, who can be against you? God will transform your life right in the presence of your enemies. Do not get discouraged woman of God; God's got you!

As I stated earlier, we are drawn by what we see. Being a person that loves beauty or is drawn to what is beautiful can be a distraction. If you are one that naturally loves beauty, as I have stated about myself, you can easily be distracted or bamboozled into the wrong direction or even the course of your life. Do not let your natural eyesight be your gauge for your future and destination.

You need spiritual eyes; you need the leading of the Holy Spirit. Do you know, when your eyes are full of light, your whole body is on track? Matthew 6:22, "The eye is the lamp of the body. If your eyes are healthy, your whole body will be full of light." The devil's agenda is to get you to gaze on something that will cause you to go into a whole different direction.

The Flesh Obscures Your Vision

Ladies, this is even in the case of that fine, handsome man that you are gazing on that God has not ordained for your life, but because you are only looking at the natural beauty and not what he has to offer you spiritually and physically—you are now off course. Let me stay right here for a minute. Some of you ladies may get in a relationship with the wrong guy because he is fine-looking and having him will appeal to your flesh nature.

You will look past the fact that he is not a God-fearing man; that he is in between jobs or has no job at all. You will excuse his staying at home with his momma and will not see that he has no ambition to get on his own, and has no goals or vision, but...because he looks good, you will settle. Your vision will be obscured by the desires of your flesh.

Having dark eyes that are not full of light can get you into a lot of trouble. When you give the devil access to your eyes, you have now given him permission to down-load all types of deception and lies into your spirit. The wrong vision will cause you to see from the devil's per-spective and not God's. There is a perfect example of this in the Bible. In the beginning, it was Adam and Eve. God gave Adam direct and clear instructions while living in the garden. God commanded Adam, "You are free to eat from any tree in the garden; but you must not eat from the tree of the knowledge of good and evil, for when you eat from it you will certainly die."

When God created Adam and Eve, He created what was good. He created them in His image and He created them to be pure; to enjoy intimacy and fellowship with Him. They did not have a care in the world! God was their protector. He was protecting them from evil; this is why He didn't want them to eat of the tree of the knowledge of good and evil. If they did so, their eyes would have been opened to the deception, errors and cunning lies of the enemy. As long as they stayed in God's presence and stayed in intimacy with Him, they wouldn't have to be worried about the spirit of deception, they wouldn't have to worry about demonic spiritual attacks.

However, once they fell into deception and their eyes were open to good and evil, then the war started be-tween their spirit and flesh. Before they ate of the tree of knowledge, there was no war going on within their members, all they knew was to follow the leading of the Spirit of God.

God was protecting them from being carnally minded. Romans 8:6 states, "For to be carnally minded is death; but to be spiritually minded is life and peace. Because the carnal mind is enmity against God: for it is not subject to the law of God, neither indeed can be." The flesh side of Adam and Eve was not given birth until they ate of the tree of knowledge and they awakened their flesh side.

How many of you know that it is the flesh that craves and desires the things of this world? They would have never known about the cravings and desires of this world if they had been obedient. Galatians 5:17, "For the flesh desires what is contrary to the Spirit, and the Spirit what is contrary to the flesh. They are in conflict with each other, so that you are not to whatever you want."

In the Garden of Eden, the flesh was dead; this was heaven on Earth. There was no sadness, pain, diseases, worries, desire to do evil; no evil was present at all, but when you are exposed to evil or the things of the world, then your flesh begins to crave those things. This is why it is important for us to be born again—repent—turn from your wicked ways; accept Jesus Christ in your life and take on His nature because as long as you gratify the flesh, and partake in the things of the world, you will desire more and more of the things that are in opposition to God.

God only wanted Adam and Eve to know what was good; He did not want them to know what was evil. There was no reason for them too because they already had it made. Just like at this very moment, God wants to give us what is good. His desire is to do you good and not evil. His desire is to give you the Kingdom and prosper you. His desire is to give you good gifts.

The devil doesn't want good for your life; he had an agenda for your life from the time you were conceived, and if he can take your vision, then he can take your purpose. The serpent (Satan) deceived Eve in the garden; his agenda was to take away her vision. The enemy wants to take away your vision too. Once he has your attention, he then manipulates you by distorting who God says you are. God told Jeremiah that he called him a prophet in his mother's womb, before he was born, and even Jeremiah doubted who God said he was. Jeremiah 1:6, "Alas, Sovereign Lord," I said, "I do not know how to speak; I am too young." Jeremiah couldn't see himself as God created Him. The enemy will highlight your weaknesses and shortcomings to you to so that you disqualify yourself.

By nature, I am an introvert and when I began to seek God on my purpose and He told me that I would preach, I was like Jeremiah. My excuse was, *"I am way too shy, and fearful to speak in front of others; I am not one that speaks in front of crowds."* I totally disregarded who He said I was, and He is the Creator! God did not care about any of my excuses, just like He didn't care about Prophet Jeremiah's. Jeremiah 1:7, "But the Lord said to me, "Do not say, "I am too young." You must go to everyone I send you to and say whatever I command you." God was not moved by Jeremiah being too young or his excuses. It was like... "Okay...and...your point being?" Who God has called, He has also equipped. God touched Jeremiah's lips and gave him the words to speak. What if Jeremiah did not obey God? I wonder what his life would have been like...

Focus on What God Has Declared

As soon as we get a glimpse or confirmation of what God called us to be, we begin to concentrate and look at what we can't do. For me, it was being too shy to speak in front of crowds. We begin to put more focus on what we *can't* do rather than on who God has declared us to be. Yes, it is a process, and there are steps to becoming mature in our God-given callings, gifts and talents, but the key is to step out. Step out and do what God tells you to do. When I prayed and asked God my purpose, and He declared preaching, I literally said, *"No I am not."* That's real funny! We tell God that we want to do His will and please Him, and will then turn around and tell Him "no" when it concerns our destiny. I could not fathom me holding a mic at all.

Well, I was in prayer one day before church and God spoke to me and said, "You are going to pray today at church." *"O boy...I don't think so!"* Please note, I had never ever prayed in front of a congregation on a mic, and here God was telling me that I was going to pray that Sunday at church. I went to church like any other Sunday, and sat towards the back. Before service was over, my pastor called up six individuals to pray, and I was one of them. He said, "Lakeea, I know there is fire in you." Only God revealed that to him because the way I prayed behind closed doors was not what I demonstrated publicly. I knew that I could not tell my pastor "no" because it would have been the same as me telling God "no" because He had already told me that I would pray that day in front of the congregation. My pastor, at the time, saw in me what I couldn't see in myself. God prompted him to call me, and He began to birth out the intercession that was already on the inside of me.

Once I stopped believing the devil's lies, I was able to step out with courage, and see myself transform before my very own eyes. The devil first feeds you with lies such as, "You will never amount to nothing, you are not equipped to do this or that, no one will ever want you, you are too stupid or you will always be in poverty." The list can go on and on. Once he speaks the lie, he will bring people or situations in your life to manifest or bring life to that lie. You begin to see the situation through your eyes, which is your perception—the lie the devil fed you. And once you begin to see things through your eyes, those perceptions will then enter into your heart and mind, causing you to be on the wrong path. Recognize that those are lies from the devil. Wash your eyes with the Word of God. Believe who God says you are, and your heart will be guarded from going in the wrong direction.

It is so important for us to have spiritual eyes because once something enters into our hearts, we tend to follow the path of our hearts. This is why David said, "Create in me a clean heart and a right spirit" because a dirty heart would lead him in the wrong direction. A heart full of God's Word, love, peace and joy will lead us down the right path, and what is in our hearts, is what is on our minds. Both your heart and mind should be in agreement with the things of God. Both your heart and mind should be in agreement with who God says you are. When we serve Him with our whole heart, mind and soul, then we are able to trust Him completely with the plan and purpose that He has for our lives.

A word of wisdom to you: When God shows you who you are in Him, and the plans and purposes He has for your life, He will then put you on someone's mind and heart. God will begin to show someone else who you are—your gifts, talents and capabilities. When this happens, do not draw back, receive who God called you to be, and walk in it. Walk through that door of opportunity that God is setting before you Woman of God! God is birthing out something new in you that others are waiting for!

I was prophesied to on many occasions regarding writing a book, but I had no idea where to start or how it would manifest. I even had one prophet ask me when was I going to write the draft of my book. At that moment, I was not ready to write a draft. I literally said, "I'm not ready to write a draft." I thought, it was going to be too much work; however, I discerned the season of the Lord upon my life and started writing in 2017. God has put an anointing on writers to write in 2017. He even began to direct me every step of the way. As I started writing, what I thought was going to be too much work was actually my passion that had been buried for a long time.

I have always had a passion to write. As I mentioned a while back, I often expressed myself and relieved my anger through writing; it was my outlet. I was a writer in so many capacities growing up and at one point during my teenage years, I even had aspirations to be a journalist and I also once tried to write a book as a little girl. I wanted to write novels. As I became an adult, the enemy distorted my vision and buried what was already on the inside of me. Now that my vision and purpose is clear, it is the time to manifest that purpose.

My Steps to Making Your Vision Clear

- It is important to feed on the Word of God. The Word of God is the Truth, and your guide to knowing what is right from wrong. Be transformed by the renewing of your mind—this is only through God's Word.

- Pay attention to the negative and toxic people around you; pay attention to the negative and toxic music you listen to; and even what you watch. All of these things shape your vision.

- As I pursued God, He gave me the discernment to know the things that were toxic to my sight.

My Prayer for You

Dear Heavenly Father, I thank you that your daughter has clear vision and that her steps are being ordered by You. I thank you that she has a discerning heart to know right from wrong. Lord, I thank you that you are revealing to her any toxic relationships, music she listens to or things that she watches that has caused her vision to be cloudy. Lord, I thank you that her eyes are good; therefore, her whole body is full of light. I pray that she will not be distracted from the things of this world that will keep her eyes off of You. I pray that her mind will be renewed daily by your Word. I pray that You will open her spiritual eyes, and give her revelations that come from Your Word. I pray that she will discern spiritual things because she has Wisdom from above. Wisdom that is pure, holy, kind; does not show partiality, peace-loving and full of mercy. Thank you Lord that she is always hungry and thirsty for You. In Jesus' Name, Amen!

Chapter 20

Your Ultimate Kingdom Assignment

Below are some principles that I have come to realize about God's plans for us. God has plans to prosper you and not to harm you—to give you a future and hope.

"For I know the plans I have for you,"
declares the LORD,
"plans to prosper you and not to harm you,
plans to give you hope and a future."
Jeremiah 29:11

You Are Unique with a Unique Calling from God

We are all called to a certain type of people or tribe, and we all have specific assignments for the Kingdom of God. We are fearfully and wonderfully made. There is not one handprint that is alike; how AMAZING is that! Your very handprint is distinctive and set apart. There is an assignment and work to do that is only going to come from your hands; you were created to build. Take a moment to think about what you were created to build. Are you created to make music, write books, create screenplays, create movies, art, dance, schools, museums, businesses, clothing, sermons, or ministries? The list can go on and on. God has given you spiritual gifts and earthly talents, and we are required to use both so that we can multiply them and bring glory to His name.

At this very moment, there may be something that you are passionate about. At this very moment, there may be a gift or talent that you are cultivating or growing in. God wants you to stay faithful in your gift and talent. Staying faithful in your gift and talent opens up doors to more gifts and talents that you never knew you had. The more I grow in God; the more He shows me about myself and the more purpose He reveals. He does not release or tell us the fullness of our purpose all at once.

He takes us on a journey and through stages. During each stage, He reveals, teaches and instructs us on what He wants us to do during that stage. The key is stepping out of the boat. God will only share so much with you, and the rest He will keep a secret until it is time.

It's Not Ability but Anointing

Have you ever had a word prophesied to you and it seemed impossible or something that you totally did not agree with because you could not see yourself doing the very thing that was spoken over your life? And because you could not see yourself as God sees you, you called the person prophesying over your life a "false prophet" because it was not confirmed in your spirit? I have been there and I would like to share the story with you.

One time, I visited a church service, and the apostle called me out and started prophesying over me that I was a psalmist and that God would put me in a church where I was able to be free in this. I totally did not receive the word of the Lord. I actually told my spiritual grandmother that I did not receive what she spoke over my life because I was not a singer in the capacity of being on the praise team or to have my own album or single. As time went on, I realized that the word she gave me had nothing to do with me being this singer on the praise team or a singer that would put out a CD.

God reminded me that I was always singing prophetically (in the shower and under the unction of the Holy Spirit). God sometimes puts prophetic songs in my spirit while I am praying. There was also a season where I would record the songs that He gave me. On one occasion, I even had an entirely different prophet call me out and ask me if I sing. I thought that was comical, and I burst out laughing, thinking, *"Here we go again with this singing ordeal."* I told him, "Yes, but I can't sing." I love to sing but not to the point where I want to join the praise team.

The prophet told me, "It's not about if you can sing; it's about the anointing." God gave me a whole new perspective when he said that. Don't get me wrong, I'm not a horrible singer; I can carry a tune. God again confirmed that word that was spoken over my life for the third time—this time through an actual demonstration.

At the time, I was leading a prayer at my church at the beginning of service and the next thing I knew, I started singing prophetically; the altar was full. I could not believe I was actually singing; the Holy Spirit took over completely. I let the Holy Spirit have His way through me; I had never sung on the mic before, and never had intentions of doing so. After I was finished, I was getting compliments from everyone, and the Glory was ALL to God!! So, I was feeling pretty good because I was complimented and encouraged on how God used me through singing (something I love to do in the shower), and my oldest son says, "Mom, did you think you were at home in the shower singing?" I couldn't do nothing but laugh! He burst my little bubble of feeling good about carrying a tune over the mic: it was the anointing, nothing but the anointing.

The Lord is Wonderful in all His ways, over time the Lord revealed that the word spoken over my life was true. I couldn't receive it at the time because I couldn't see it in myself. Even if God had revealed it to me first, I still would have denied it, as if I can tell the Creator (Jesus Christ) about what He created. No matter how the word would have come, I would have questioned it, and He would have had to have confirmed it like He did.

Know Your Times and Seasons: The Issachar Anointing

There are some words that we receive that are for a set time; pray about the word spoken over your life. If it is a curse or ill-spoken word, do not agree with it and come out of agreement with it immediately. God will give you the discernment and insight to know what is outright demonic, but you stay in prayer and seek His face daily.

Anything that does not line up with His Word is definitely demonic and do not come under agreement with anything that is contrary to the Word of God. Know your season to begin a thing and end a thing—this is called the Issachar anointing.

There is a set time for you to move forward in what God has called you to do; timing is everything. You do not want to miss your season or go into your season too early—both can be detrimental. Missing your season will cause you to have a delay, and can cause you to be content and stagnate, which in turn delays the deliverance and breakthrough in the individuals you are assigned to. Moving into your season too early, without proper preparation, can cause you to encounter spiritual attacks that you are not ready to face and can cause you to be under unwanted burdens and stress. These can cause you to negatively affect those that you are called to, and could ultimately kill you spiritually. Yield to the prompting of the Holy Spirit; there are people that are waiting for you to move forward in your God-given gifts and talents.

Courage and Boldness Comes As You Move Forward

As you pursue and move forward in the things of God, He will begin to release courage and boldness over your life. Courage and boldness only comes by stepping out and doing the thing that is uncomfortable—the thing(s) you fear.

I naturally do not like speaking in front of crowds, but the more I do it, the more comfortable I have become with it. I still get nervous at times depending on what I am doing, but I do not allow that to stop me from going forth, because He will not leave me alone.

God Looks at the Heart, Not the Outward Appearance

Sometimes we fear moving forward because we do not want to mess up and we are looking for perfection. I have been there. The truth is, when you are a perfectionist, you are most likely insecure, have rejection issues, a people-pleaser and driven by performance.

Yes, I was all four. If I made a mistake, I would be so hard on myself and would wonder and worry over what people thought of me. But when you begin to be confident in who God called you to be, you are no longer driven by people. You begin to understand that God is not moved by performance, which is also a religious spirit. He is not moved by your outer appearance when it comes to who He chooses for a Kingdom assignment—it is the heart that He sees. As God said to Samuel, "But the LORD said to Samuel, "Do not consider his appearance or his height, for I have rejected him. The LORD does not look at the things people look at. People look at the outward appearance, but the LORD looks at the heart." (Samuel 16:7)

Perfectionists also have critical spirits. They are critical of other's mistakes, and are always sizing up someone else's actions to see how well they did or did not perform. Do not misunderstand me; you are responsible for being prepared and living a disciplined life, but even in that, you will make mistakes, but your mistakes are not enough for God to count you out or put you out of the game. His rules are different from the world's rules.

This is why it is so important to humble yourself under God's mighty hand and allow Him to promote you in every area of your life because when He puts you on an assignment and you mess up, He will continue to elevate you in the presence of your enemies. Your enemies are sizing up your failures and mistakes, but it's just a perfect opportunity for God to demonstrate His glory in your life and reward you with a great victory!

Proverbs 24:17-18 says, "Do not gloat when your enemy falls; when they stumble, do not let your heart rejoice, or the Lord will see and disapprove and turn his wrath away from them." Did you catch that verse? You may have some enemies that are rejoicing because you fell, because you stumbled or made a mistake, but just because they are rejoicing, God is going to turn the situation around right in front of them.

See Your Losses and Mistakes As Victories

I have some advice for you. Begin to look at your losses or mistakes as great comebacks; as great victories. Do not be concerned about what someone is thinking of you. Stop being concerned if he or she affirms or validates you. Do not worry about their faces. God told the prophet Jeremiah to not fear their faces and speak what God tells him to speak, God goes on to say, "If you fear them, then I will shame you in front of them."

God will embarrass you, for real, when you seek to please men over pleasing and obeying God. Jeremiah

1:17, "Get up and prepare for action. Go out and tell them everything I tell you to say. Do not be afraid of them, or I will make you look foolish in front of them." When you obey God, He has your back. It doesn't matter what people say or do—He is there upholding you, and you cannot be touched because no weapon formed against you shall prosper.

In Jeremiah 1:8, God tells Jeremiah to not be afraid of them because He is with him and will rescue him. And God is with you to rescue you too. When you begin to truly believe that God has your back, you will not measure yourself by works, but by faith. Your faith—belief that will move you into the things of God. Your faith will cause you to obey even when you see their faces, even when you feel like you are not equipped for the work that He has for you to do.

You Are Fearfully and Wonderfully Made—Believe Him

Begin to believe in who God says you are. If you are still trying to figure out who you are in God, just believe that you are someone great with a lot to offer because God has said that you are fearfully and wonderfully made, and God does not create junk—He declared what He created as good. It's up to you to discover what that good is. Draw near to God and He will draw near to you and reveal it to you.

I really feel like a lot of people hesitate to move forward because of unbelief and fear of failing. It is often hard for people to fathom being who God declared them to be because of their current state. As a people, we sometimes repeat things because it sounds good or because it's a popular cliché. The cliché, "You need to believe in yourself" is a subtle trick and seed of deception that the enemy plants in the hearts and minds of people. I would say, "Stop believing in yourself and believe in God—believe Him!" I know the world says, "Just believe in your-self." Well, that can sometimes be the problem...you are trying to believe and trust in yourself.

You can't even save yourself by your works. You can't say to God, "Okay, let me clean myself up first, let me get myself together before I accept you in my life." It is impossible for you to save yourself. He accepts you when you accept Him, and He does the cleaning up. God brings forth the increase of sanctification, holiness and righteousness in your life, not you. It was through God's grace—unmerited favor—that you are saved. If you had the capability of saving yourself, then you would have something to boast about and be full of pride! You would be saying, "Yep, I did that, look at me"... while popping your collar. God would not get any credit, which is totally prideful, and God hates pride.

The thing that God created you to do, that is bigger than you and takes a big God to accomplish. It's not in your ability to accomplish it and it's not meant to be in your ability, otherwise you would take the credit and the glory. So, when you are believing in yourself, you are being proud; you are believing that it takes you to accomplish that thing.

You Can Do All Things Through Christ Who Gives You Strength

Rejection will open the door for pride, and pride brings dishonor—not honor. The enemy wants to bring dishonor to your life through any means that he can. Paul stated in Philippians that he could do ALL things through Christ who gave him strength. Paul did not say, "I can do all things through my own strength." Paul looked to Christ to be able to do the things that appeared to be impossible; that appeared to be hard to do. Paul was able to maintain his composure and forwardness in Christ whether he was full or hungry, living in plenty or want. God's grace gives us the power to accomplish what we can't do on our own. God will give you the supernatural ability to accomplish every work that He has set out for you to do; He will give you the supernatural strength to do it.

Why? Because you are HIS masterpiece; HIS prize possession; HIS creation, and HE shares His glory with no man. God is not going to allow you to brag and boast over something that He predestined; that HE created. He wants all of the glory out of your life, so God will allow you to be weak in areas so HE can display HIS strength, anointing and power through you. "But he said to me, "My grace is sufficient for you, for my power is made perfect in weakness." Therefore, I will boast all the more gladly about my weaknesses, so that Christ's power may rest on me." 2 Cor 12:9.

Moses had a stuttering problem and God called him to be a deliverer to the Israelites. God used Moses' weakness to show that it was only through God and by God that he would be able to deliver the Israelites. The prophet Jeremiah thought he was too young, but again, God wanted to display His glory by showing that HIS Glory is not determined by age, gender or anything else.

God uses the foolish things of the world to confound the wise; those that have a worldly system and worldly wisdom or way of thinking—a philosophical thinking pattern. Our weaknesses show that we cannot believe in ourselves. This is why it is so important to stay humble, especially after God exalts you. You must always remember that it was He who brought you out of that place you were once in. God constantly reminded the Israelites to not forget who brought them out of Egypt. He consistently reminded them to not forget who gave them the power to obtain wealth. Do not forget Him when He releases the floodgates of favor over your life, and always believe Him—and not yourself!

Esteem Others Better Than Yourself

It is also important to esteem others better than yourself. Praising the glory of God that is demonstrated and revealed in others also keeps you humble. It keeps the word "I" or "me" out of your vocabulary. Individuals that do not know how to celebrate others are also insecure and have a spirit of jealousy. When you are not able to celebrate and esteem others better than yourself, you are essentially saying that you do not believe that God has placed value in you. You are saying that you want the attention, and love the focus to be on you, which means you need your rejection to be pacified and you are possibly going through abandonment issues.

Nowadays, it is very easy for me to compliment and genuinely be excited for others, but there was a time when I placed so much value on what people thought of me, that if I was not getting enough attention I felt that something was wrong with me, and often felt rejected.

I was putting my trust and affirmation in man before God. The enemy knew I carried a spirit of rejection; so, he would place situations and false things that appeared to be real in my life to water that seed of rejection. I eventually began to recognize the enemy's tactics and would cast him down every time I saw him working through people and situations. There was a time that if I felt that I was not accepted, I would intentionally not form or engage in certain relationships. I began to recognize the enemy's tactic and would do the opposite. I would intentionally engage because I refused to let the enemy continue to make the spirit of rejection stronger. It was time for him to lose his grip.

If you are experiencing the spirit of rejection, it should be cast out—but that is not enough. It is important to maintain your deliverance. I was able to maintain my deliverance by staying connected to individuals that did not have a spirit of rejection; by staying connected to people that walked in boldness and courage; by staying connected to individuals that are comfortable in who they are and in being themselves. Seeing those types of people operate in the things of God with favor, prosperity and success was an impartation to my life.

Being connected to the right people is always key in maintaining your deliverance. If you need more boldness, stay connected to those that walk in their authority with boldness and courage; this is the same for fear. If you have fear, stay connected to the bold and powerful. If you need to maintain deliverance from severe depression, stay connected to those that walk in joy, happiness and have a gift of humor. Whatever you need, you need to stay connected. Connections can come through personal relationships, books, Periscope, or YouTube. Growth and elevation comes through staying connected to the right people.

You have been so conditioned to put your trust more in man and what they think of you, that you strive to please man and not God. Galatians 1:10, "Am I now trying to win the approval of human beings, or of God? Or am I trying to please people? If I were still trying to please people, I would not be a servant of Christ. Galatians 1:10 is very clear, pleasing people is not for a servant of Christ, but we should strive to please Him.

Whatever you do, serve the Lord graciously and with a pure, sincere heart. God will not turn His back on you or remove the assignment from you because you made a mistake; He will not be angry with you or cast you aside as an orphan. He understands that we will make mistakes. Just like a baby wobbles and falls when he is learning to walk, so we will also stumble at times when we are walking in something new. He understands that and when we are weak—He is made strong so that His glory is shown.

For example, you may have to speak in front of an audience and mess up on your words or totally forget your next thought out of nervousness. It's okay. God called you and He affirms you. He will not disqualify you, and guess what? Those that gloat or look down upon you because you made a mistake while going forward in your assignment will also see the glory and hand of God upon your life as He elevates you. They will not be able to deny that God is with you; He will set a table in the presence of your enemies.

It's Time to Mature

I am at the point in my life that I do not worry about who likes me or what others are saying about me because I know what my Father thinks of me. He has affirmed me; He has validated me. He has affirmed and validated you too; you are His daughter. Man can't take away what God gives you. People will always be curious about what they don't know—let them be curious, keep your eyes on Jesus and strive for His perfection!

His perfection means to be complete; to become mature in the things of God so you can take on His image. It's time to become mature in your prayer life; it's time to become mature in the Word of God; it's time to become mature in your character. It's time to become mature in your God-given gifts and talents. In order to mature, you must have discipline; you must strive, just as an athlete strives to improve in his or her sport. Maturity does not happen in complacency or stagnation. You must make a conscious effort to do what your body sometimes does not feel like doing. Push pass the way you are feeling and even the negative thoughts in your mind. Practice and preparation reaps maturity (perfection in the things of God).

You must beat your body daily as Paul stated in I Corinthians 9:27, "I discipline my body like an athlete, training it to do what it should. Otherwise, I fear that after preaching to others I myself might be disqualified." We have a responsibility to train our bodies. This Scripture tells me that our bodies do not automatically conform to the things that we want it to do; we don't just wake up one day and we are in shape physically or spiritually. The responsibility lies in us, and grace kicks in to help us to accomplish that discipline.

My Prayer for You

Dear Heavenly Father, thank you for the Woman of God reading this prayer. Thank you, Lord, that she is walking in boldness, and the confidence of the Holy Spirit. Thank you, Jesus, that she is courageous. Thank you, Lord, that You have not given her a spirit of fear, but of power, love and a sound mind. Thank you, Jesus, that she is as bold as a lion. Thank you, Lord, that You have given her a voice that changes atmospheres in every area of her life. Lord, I thank you that she is walking in influence and authority, and not fear. Thank you, Lord, that you are helping her in every area that she is weak and growing her in those areas daily. Thank you, Lord, that your grace is sufficient in her weakness. Lord, I thank you that she is not allowing her lack of skill or inabilities to cause her to not move in the purpose and plan that you have for her life. Thank you, Lord, for the love that you are showing her and will continue to show as she trusts in You. In Jesus' Name, Amen!

Chapter 21

Being Called to Rejection: A New Perspective

Rejected by the World

When growing up from a little girl to my adult years, I always felt like I was different and misunderstood. Something on the inside of me was always telling me that I was created for purpose—that I was created for something that was not mediocre. It was the Holy Spirit speaking to me. In my core, I felt that I was bigger than my current circumstance, environments and jobs. There were times that I literally felt in my spirit that I needed to break out and be free—be free in who God called me to be. It was as if I was bound and God was calling me to more, but I just did not know how. How do I become free? How do I break out of these prison walls? I felt the greatness on the inside of me, and then began to hear the words: "greatness is on the inside of you." I wanted to move into the greatness that God was proclaiming over my life. I wanted to experience EVERYTHING that He had, and still has, for me.

During the time that I did not fully give myself over to the Lord, I still maintained a connection with Him. I wasn't living a surrendered life, but I knew He existed. I had a Bible that was called a Promise Bible. I absolutely loved that Bible because it broke down the Scriptures in a way that I could understand. I often carried that Bible around with me to friends' houses because of the excitement over what I learned. I often shared the goodness of Jesus while still living in sin; and those that I hung out with were living in sin too—but I carried Him with me.

175

In the middle of my sin, I carried destiny on the inside of me. I was preaching sermons, witnessing and sharing Scriptures; I couldn't stop talking about God. That was a sure sign that He was calling me out of darkness; calling me out of the world into His marvelous light. If you find yourself preaching sermons and talking about the goodness of Jesus while you are sinning, that is a sure sign that you are called and set apart for a purpose in Jesus Christ. You need to go ahead and surrender—and give a "YES!"

I did not have any plans on getting saved. I had a relative that was always inviting me to church; he was always calling me. It got to the point that I stopped answering my phone; I would let the voicemail pick up. I got tired of him calling me every week to go to church. My answer was always "no." On top of that, my mom was always saying "you need to go to church."

My thing was, I did not want to be playing church or playing with God. I knew in my heart of hearts that I was not ready to give up the lifestyle that I was living. I knew that I would have just been a churchgoer with no intentions on changing. I knew that once I left church; I was going to lay up with my boyfriend, or go to the drug spot to be with him. I didn't want to play both sides of the fence— that was very hypocritical to me and I did not like hypocrisy. Either I was going to live for Jesus—or not; there was no in between— it was all or nothing. So, when I turned my life totally over to God, I was all in. Whatever He wanted to do in my life, I was all for it. I was willing to let Him take total control; I was wide open!

As I journeyed with God, I eventually started being told things such as, "You think you are 'holier-than-thou'."— which left me totally confused! How could I be 'holier-than-thou' when I was merely speaking what the Scriptures were saying? My thoughts were, "God said it, not me." I believe those that rejected me because of my belief in Jesus Christ were experiencing conviction. Most likely, they did not appreciate the fact that I did not continue to give them a justification to keep sinning.

Accepted by God

I was beginning to get closer and closer to Jesus Christ in my relationship with Him. I was falling in love with Him, and the more I learned of Him, the more of my true identity in Christ was coming through. He was sanctifying me and removing the old man. Those that were calling me 'holier-than-thou' were not pursuing God or in relationship with Him at the level I was during that time, therefore my light was shining on their darkness, causing them to reject the holiness of Jesus Christ.

The closer I got to God, the more my discernment and conscience was heightened. I could discern the things that God was not pleased with. The closer I got to Him, the more He started to refine me. He started taking away a lot of the things that I liked to watch; the music I liked to listen to. He even changed the way I dressed. I recall turning on the T.V. one day (I am not a big T.V. watcher), and I was watching this reality show. It was a reality show that I watched every week, and this particular time, I started getting disgusted by the language and content. The language and content never bothered me before: God gave me new ears and new eyes. He did not want to contaminate the oil that He was releasing over my life.

There was another time that a friend and I went wine tasting. We hit almost every wine tasting spot between Battle Creek and Jackson. I was feeling pretty good; it was my first wine tasting adventure. When I got home, and opened my Bible (I wasn't looking for any particular passage to read), I opened up to a Scripture on drinking alcohol. I closed my Bible and opened it back up for a second time, and there was another Scripture on drinking alcohol. The Holy Spirit convicted me that He was not pleased, and I was not going to continue in something that He was not pleased with, so I immediately stopped—no question.

If the Holy Spirit is convicting you to stop doing something, just stop. Don't continue because when you ignore Him and continue, you harden your heart and your ability to discern or know when something is right or wrong.

The same thing happened to me with fornication. I was fornicating one night (yes, I was a fornicator), and I had to stop in the middle of the act because I began to feel so unclean and dirty. I literally felt unclean; it was not a good feeling. I jumped up and said, "I can't do this anymore." I was in a committed relationship and told him that I could no longer fornicate.

The Holy Spirit started convicting me in every area of my life. I couldn't even go into the clubs anymore without feeling the same conviction. I would start having thoughts like, *"What if Jesus comes back right now? I am going to Hell."* I would literally feel the demonic presence that was around me. My convictions were beginning to get real, and I could not resist because I was open to receive.

Once I gave Him permission, He started doing the work. I developed a friendship with the Lord, and my dedication to Him caused me to be rejected even more. It began the journey of our friendship. I remember God telling me, "Your life has now begun." In other words, I did not have life until I met Him. He would wake me up in the wee hours of the morning to talk to me. He would teach me things that I never knew; the unfolding of the revelations from His Word inspired me to keep pursuing Him as He pursued me. It was amazing to experience Him like I did. It got to the point, where some days, I would want to hang out with my other Christian friends, and the Lord would say, "No stay home and spend time with me," or sometimes I would want to go shopping for the day, and He would say, "No, stay home and spend time with me."

I felt like God was requiring so much from me. I would look at other Christians and think, *"Why do they get to do this or that?"* I felt like a child that tells his parent, "So and so gets to do this or that, so why can't I?" I started communicating to God in the same way. He was taking me higher. It felt as if He was requiring more of me, and I was open to receive His impartation of holiness. The purpose on my life required a higher level of responsibility, and He was preparing me.

He is requiring more of you too. You have to be open to receive and obey, even in those times that you want to do something, and what you want to do may not necessarily be bad; He is testing your obedience. The more you obey God, the more your ears are tuned to His voice. Obedience brings clarity and wisdom.

Rejection—The New Perspective

Your obedience to pick up your cross and follow Christ will cause you to be rejected, and not just by non-believers. I could understand the rejection I was receiving from those that were not saved or living for Jesus Christ, but it was puzzling to me to be rejected by those that called themselves saved. I felt misunderstood and rejected for living a sold-out life for Christ. We were supposed to be on the same team; serving the same God, but yet me being sold-out for Jesus caused me to be rejected. God began to reveal to me that He called me to rejection. I know this sounds a little strange, but I will explain.

I had experienced the demonic spirit of rejection from childhood that caused missed opportunities, a delay in my destiny, people pleasing, anger, bitterness, unforgiveness, shame, doubt, fear, uncertainties, the spirit of offense, being defensive, and the lack of trust and being suspicious of people. This type of demonic spirit of rejection brought all of his friends with him. This is not the type of rejection that I am referring to. God never called me to "fit in" or people please—He called me to be set apart. He was calling me to Himself to fulfill a Kingdom assignment on the Earth that was not determined by whether people accepted it or not.

Now that is a Word right there: The Kingdom assignment that God has called you to do on the Earth does not need the validation from people or the acceptance of people. Who do you serve? God or man? Lecrae stated it perfectly, "If you live for people's acceptance you will die from their rejection." John 12:43 says, "For they loved human praise more than praise from God." Galatians 1:10, "Am I now trying to win the approval of human beings, or of God? Or am I trying to please people, I would not be a servant of Christ." Being a servant of Christ will cause you to be rejected.

The demonic spirit of rejection was interfering with my relationship with Jesus Christ. It was clouding my ability to see who I am in Christ. It was clouding my ability to see that God was not calling me to have man's approval. During Jesus' life on Earth, He was rejected on many occasions, yet He still sought to do the Father's Will. He did not sugarcoat His message or tell a lie to gain followers; He kept it one hundred during His entire ministry. The Jews did not believe He was the Son of God, and He could only perform a few miracles in His hometown among His relatives. Jesus kept it moving and never stopped with His assignment.

Jesus' message was offensive to some. In John Chapter 6, Jesus had many disciples to desert Him because they were not willing to eat of His flesh and drink of His blood. They were not willing to die to their ways to serve Him with their whole heart, mind, soul and strength. This seemed too hard for them, but little did they know is that with Christ, all things are possible. Jesus was not moved because He lost followers; those that received His Word were the ones that followed Him. Do not be concerned about who has walked out of your life or who does not understand your relationship with Jesus Christ. When they reject you, they are actually rejecting Jesus in you. You have been called to rejection for righteousness' sake.

If your message or lifestyle in Jesus Christ is never offensive or causes some persecution, then you may be operating in the demonic spirit of rejection. Let your light shine so others can see the good works of Jesus Christ in your life. Some will be fans and some will be followers. It is not for you to divide your message and water the truth or your lifestyle to please others, it is for you to present your body as a living sacrifice—holy and acceptable unto Jesus Christ. Persecution for righteousness' sake is what brings the glory of God. If there is no suffering, then there is no glory. If Jesus was rejected, you too will be rejected!

My Steps to Dealing with Rejection and Persecution

- Looking at the life of Jesus has helped me to accept rejection and persecution for living right.

- Begin to read the gospels of Jesus Christ, in Matthew, Mark, Luke and John. As you see His life of persecution, you will then see that you are not exempt from persecution.

- Read the Scriptures lined up with the Word concerning persecution.

My Prayer for You

Dear Heavenly Father, I thank you that the Woman of God that is reading this prayer is not walking in a spirit of compromise because she is being rejected for righteousness' sake. Thank you, Lord, that she is standing on the Word of God and always has an answer for the hope that lies within her. You said in your Word that the Spirit of the Lord rests on those that are persecuted for righteousness' sake. Blessed are those that have been persecuted for righteousness' sake, for the Kingdom of Heaven is theirs. Thank you, Jesus, that she is blessed for doing what is right. Thank you, Lord, that she seeks her praise from You and not man. Thank you, Lord, that her life is bringing glory to Your name and Your name only. Thank you, Lord, that you approve her and it is You that is bringing increase in her life. Thank you, Lord, that she is walking in the good works that you predestined for her before the foundation of the world. In Jesus' Name, Amen!

Chapter 22

A Life of Excellence

The Prophet Daniel is an excellent role model for the Kingdom of God. He did not compromise or bow down to idols, and he had a disciplined lifestyle. He prayed three times a day, and maintained a life of fasting. He maintained his relationship with God by putting his body under subjection, and strengthening his spiritual muscles. Even though he served under a number of earthly kings, he viewed himself as a servant of God and depended on God in all that he did.

When Jesus saves you and you surrender, it doesn't stop there. It is a journey of walking with Him and learning from Him. As I have spoken about previously, His Spirit will begin to lead and guide you towards greater levels of holiness. He will encourage and empower you to be disciplined in every area of your life. He will enable you to lay a solid foundation—so let Him lead and guide you!

TransHERmation is about becoming disciplined in areas that you were once undisciplined. God has designed us with a body, a soul (our thoughts and emotions) and a spirit; and they are intricately connected. Just as much as we need TransHermation spiritually, we need it mentally and physically. The rest of this chapter will focus on some practical tips for your TransHERmation journey.

TransHERmation Physically

Some of the common excuses that people have for not maintaining a consistent devotion of prayer to Jesus Christ, or a consistent life of reading His Word are "I'm too tired, or I get too sleepy." I do believe that there are times when a demonic spirit is involved when a person gets tired or sleepy every time they pray or read the Word. However, I am going to add another perspective to this. Sometimes the lack of energy and focus towards the things of God can depend on your physical lifestyle.

Sometimes the reason why you can't pray or read the Word, is because you are too stressed, too tired and have no energy. Your physical lifestyle will have an impact on your spiritual lifestyle.

The Prophet Daniel maintained a lifestyle of excellence with his health. There was a certain diet that he maintained, and I bet he exercised too. I don't really know if he exercised or not because the Bible does not state that, but we do know he maintained a certain eating lifestyle. I am not saying that it is bad to eat certain foods because God has declared all food good, as long as we pray and bless our food. We are not under the old law. However, God makes us all individually and differently, and if eating pork is causing you to have high blood pressure, then stop eating pork.

If you are having difficulty controlling the amount you are eating, you are operating out of a spirit of gluttony. If you want to go to the next level in TransHERmation, it is not going to happen. I have to keep it real with you. Gluttony leads to poverty, and with poverty can come depression and anger. If you are overweight and cannot function because of it, how are you going to have enough energy and tenacity to pour into the people that God has assigned you to? But it's not all about being overweight. You can be skinny and not have the energy that you need to move in the things of God because you are not eating correctly.

The places and assignments that God declares over your life are going to require you to be in shape—both spiritually and physically. There is a level of God's glory that He wants to demonstrate and carry through you. But if your physical body is too weak to handle it, then you will give up easily on your assignment. You will begin to go back to the same statement, "I'm too tired," "This is too much."

God anoints us for specific assignments, but in that assignment, you are using your physical body to carry out that assignment.

If you are not healthy, then you will only be able to go so far in your assignment. I am going to give you an example. Let's say you are called to be a Psalmist, and a part of being a Psalmist is to be the worship leader. Well, when you are a worship leader, you are not sitting down on the stage ushering God's Spirit in, you are standing up and making movements. If you are unhealthy or all out of shape, you will only be able to carry the people so far. There are plenty of examples that I could give in this area, but wanted to give only one. If you are experiencing some type of physical limitation that would prevent you from doing what the average person can do, do something—whatever you are able to do, do it, use whatever God has given you.

Your body also needs proper rest and sleep. Your brain needs to be revived; and mental clarity and memory depends on proper sleep. Without proper sleep, rest, diet and exercise, you can begin to open yourself up to a spirit of mental confusion. This type of confusion from a lack of rest causes you to have mental blockages, memory loss, cloudy thoughts, headaches and anxiety. The lack of proper rest and sleep can also cause unwanted stress in your life.

Some of you are not getting sufficient rest and sleep because you are trying to do assignments that God has NOT called you to. Some of you are busy bodies, busy for nothing and accomplishing nothing because you are trying to solve problems that God did not assign you to solve. You are carrying burdens you should not be carrying—false burdens—which cause you to be physically drained and tired.

Some of you will stay up late and rise early because you are busy operating out of selfish ambition. I do not believe God demands an assignment on us so heavy that He would require us to labor, day in and day out, without the proper sleep and rest that we need to continue to have the mental clarity to finish that assignment. As a matter of fact, look at what the Word of God says: Psalm 127:2, "In vain you rise early and stay up late, toiling for food to eat – for He grants sleep to those He loves." This Scripture clearly tells us that He grants us sleep! The question to ask yourself is—is God telling you to stay up late? What are your motivations? Is it more about you, or advancing God's Kingdom? If it is not ordered by God, then it is most likely your own selfish ambition.

Make sure you are looking after yourself physically. Eat a healthy diet, get sufficient rest and sleep. As you begin to have greater mental clarity, you will be able to hear the Holy Spirit speaking to you clearly; you will be able to hear and know your Father's voice.

Excellence of Appearance

When you can hear God clearly, now you are open to hear what He says about you. You can now hear Him calling you princess, queen, jewel or my beautiful daughter. It is something about a Father validating His daughter. When your Father validates and affirms you, you begin to have a boldness and courage about yourself that you didn't have before. It begins to show outwardly.

A woman of TransHERmation that has been changed inwardly will begin to change outwardly. The way she dresses will change; her appetite for the things of the world will change. Her hairstyle may even change—some of you will actually start to comb your hair. You may treat yourself every now and then to a new outfit or new shoes. You might get your nails done; a pedicure; or maybe even a facial or massage. A woman of TransHERmation values herself enough to change her image outwardly.

Changing your image outwardly does not mean that you have to be wearing name brand or expensive clothes or jewelry. It means you know who you are and that you belong to a royal priesthood. Some of you do not care about your outer appearance because you have not placed value on yourself. One of the things that I used to always say when I was living in the world was, "You have to always be ready." In other words, you never know who you will run into. Single ladies, you might run into your Boaz, but if you never comb your hair, or put some clothes on or look decent, then you have made yourself unapproachable. Don't get me wrong, the purpose of TransHERmation outwardly is not all about catching your Boaz, but as I said, it can play a part (wink-wink).

How you carry yourself outwardly is a reflection of who you belong to. I have often heard people say, "Man looks at the outer appearance and God looks at the heart." They have taken this Scripture to mean that it doesn't matter how they physically dress. They have taken this Scripture to mean, "It's okay if I don't iron my clothes, it's okay if I look slouchy, or don't clean my nails, or it's okay if I don't buy new shoes and stop wearing the ones with holes in them; it's okay if I always wear rags on my head and go to the grocery store with my pajamas on." No, no, no! Woman of TransHERmation, this should not be so! Yes, you are correct in saying that God looks at the heart, and man the outer appearance. There you go—the people that you will encounter as you walk in the new you will be looking at your outer appearance because they do not know your heart as God does, and some of the people that you will encounter and even do business with, will not be saved with Jesus Christ as their Lord and personal Savior. There are people from high places that God wants to connect you with; there are deals, contracts and new positions that God has for you, and if you are not valuing yourself, you may get overlooked.

Remember when I applied for an Administrative position, and the manager at the time told me that he had no idea that I had a bachelor's degree and master's level coursework under my belt because I wore uniforms and transported patients to their appointments for a living. Again, he measured my abilities and skills based on my outer appearance. He had no idea of my skill set or capabilities until he had an actual conversation with me. When I made that prophetic declaration over my life, came out of those uniforms and began to dress business casual because that was where I wanted to go—God did promote me. I had to change my mindset. and believe that I was destined for greater—greater than my current position. I dressed to reflect that change in mindset. There is a level of respect that you receive when you begin to operate in boldness and courage through Jesus Christ.

I challenge you to make a prophetic declaration over your life, and declare over your life what God has called you to be. Begin to declare: I am a millionaire; I am an entrepreneur; I have my own business; I am promoted; I am a person of influence; I am operating in the gift of the spirit that God called me to with boldness; whatever you need to declare, declare it! And girlfriend, go buy yourself a new outfit, treat yourself to a pedicure, put on some lip gloss if you don't wear make-up, go get your hair done. Don't worry about going to buy something expensive if you can't afford it because one thing about a woman, we can make a $20 outfit look like a million bucks; especially, if you add some beautiful accessories to it. I guarantee you; you are going to feel fabulous!

You are beautiful, fearfully and wonderfully made! Adorn yourself with the Love of Jesus first and foremost, and then let Him shower you with His goodness and favor through the manifestation of your outward beauty.

TransHERmation—Investing in You

A part of TransHERmation is investment—investing in yourself. When you value yourself, it is easy for you to invest in yourself, and you will reap a return for investing in you! When you are being transformed, you have to work on, and change the broke and poverty-stricken mentality. I will be brave enough to say that if you are not willing to give something, then you are not ready to receive something. You cannot get a return unless you sow some seed. Think on that for a minute.

You must give something in order to receive something. Some of you want to elevate yourselves, but you are not willing to purchase a book or books, watch a webinar, sign up for a training, or support others by investing in their ministry to get what you need. If you are called to be an entrepreneur and have no real knowledge in this area, then you should be on the lookout for some Kingdom entrepreneurs that have the training that you can benefit from. If you want to write a book or self-publish a book, you should be purchasing books on how to self-publish and connect to others that have been through the process. Whatever you need, God has someone in the Kingdom that you can invest in to get the knowledge you need.

I just talked about it being okay to buy yourself a new outfit, get a new hairdo or new shoes. Well, some of you have no problem buying yourself something new to wear, but have a problem with investing in knowledge that will assist you with where you need to go.

Prior to writing this book, I felt in my spirit and declared prophetically over my life that I would have coaches and mentors in my life to assist me in the areas that I was weak or needed more knowledge for growth. I didn't know how I was going to receive the knowledge, but God declared over my life that I was going on a season of learning and growth.

He also declared that I was going to write my first book. God began to lead me to other men and women in the Kingdom of God that were offering training and coaching in the areas that I wanted elevation.

I didn't hesitate or think twice about signing up for the training because I knew it was a manifestation of what He had already spoken. For writing the book, Prophetess Sophia Ruffin, hosted *Complete The Book in 10 Days* coaching webinar, and Apostle John Eckhardt offered a *WriteIt 2017* training. Tiphani Montgomery offered *Kingdom Entrepreneur University* for entrepreneurs or inspiring entrepreneurs. Prophetess Kisha Cephas offered *The Crushing* mentorship program, and the *Crushing of a Prophet* mentorship program; also, Apostle Mike Hathaway offered *Wealth Creation Academy*. I did not hesitate to invest because they had the expertise and knowledge that I needed to go to the next level in my spiritual and physical ministry.

Stop right now and read I Kings 17:7-16. God sent Elijah to a poor widow woman for bread. God could have sent Elijah to a rich wealthy woman, but He sent Elijah to a poor widow. The widow told Elijah that she only had enough for herself and her son. Elijah instructed her to go make some bread for him first, and what was left over, she had to prepare for herself and her son. Elijah gave the widow the Word of the Lord, that there will always be enough left in her containers until the time comes for it to rain on the land again. The widow did not hesitate to make Elijah some bread first. God sent Elijah to a poor woman for food because not only did he need what she had, but she needed what he had. The widow was able to have enough bread until it rained on the land. Not only did the widow have enough bread, but her son was healed. Read the story. The Bible says that when you receive a prophet, you will receive a prophet's reward. When you receive a righteous person, you will receive a righteous person's reward.

Some of you are too prideful to invest because you may be focusing on the person that God has called you to invest in, so that you can reap a return. You may be saying, "They are already wealthy or well to do, so why would I invest in them?" You know why? Because you need what they have. The poor widow needed what Elijah had, just as much as he needed what she had. There are times when you are stuck and not able to go to the next level because you lack the knowledge and impartation needed to go to the next level. Do yourself a favor, and invest in "you!"

TransHERmation—Practical Credit Score Booster Tips

As I mentioned before, when you are being transformed, you have to work on, and change your broke and poverty-stricken mentality. However, along with addressing your mental attitude towards money, you have to physically work on your credit score. You cannot invest money if you are in debt. I have been there and have the following tips to help you recover:

- Make sure you are not using over 30% of your total credit card limit. Lenders will see you as a risk because you have nearly used all of your credit card limits, which in turn could make it difficult for you to afford to pay for another credit card or loan.

- Request an increase on your credit card limit. Doing so will lower your credit utilization.

- Transfer money from one credit to another that has lower interest rates.

- If you now have decent or good credit, but have a loan or credit card with high interest rates due to a time that you did not have good credit, apply for a loan that will now offer you lower interest rates to pay off the previous high interest loans or credit cards. It is better to be paying on a low interest loan with lower payments, than a high interest loan with higher payments. That's my take on it, at least.

- If you have no credit at all, but want to establish credit, you can do a few things. Do you know someone that you can trust and KNOW has good credit; and KNOW pays their bill on time; and you KNOW will not jack up the credit limit to the max? If you do, you can get on their credit card(s) to help boost your credit. They are responsible for the card and making the payments, but you are gaining the advantage of raising your score. For the parents out there that are credit responsible, put your 18-year-old on your credit card—to establish their credit early on, but do not give them the credit card, they most likely are not responsible enough yet, unless you train them early. By putting your teenager on your credit card, they will end up in the 700+ very quickly. Of course, they must build their credit history, but this is a great start for them. Secondly, get an unsecured credit card to build your credit.

- PAY YOUR BILLS! PAY YOUR BILLS! PAY YOUR BILLS—ON TIME! Paying your bills late or not at all will cause your credit score to drop.

- Start paying off the high interest credit cards first, but if you must, start paying off lower amounts owed, then by all means do it!

- Do not have too many credit cards!! Your goal should be to get to a place where you don't need the credit cards; just for the purpose of establishing credit.

- Do not carry high credit card limits in your purse because then you will be tempted to pull it out to buy unnecessary things.

- Consider consolidating your loans that will give you a lower interest rate and lower payment.

- If you are debating paying off credit cards or loans first to boost your credit, pay off credit cards first. Having low or zero balances on credit cards boosts your credit score much faster than paying off a loan first. However, if you are financially able, pay them all off: Debt-Free is the goal! God wants us to get free spiritually and physically. Let's get free, and stay free!

My Prayer for You

Lord, I thank you for the Woman of God that is going on her own journey of TransHERmation. I thank you that she is transforming both spiritually and physically. I thank you that she is taking some time out for herself; whether that is going to get a massage, her hair done, a pedicure, a new outfit, or on a nice walk. I thank you Lord that she is not neglecting herself from receiving favor and blessing in her life that will also come physically. I thank you Lord that there is not one area in her life that is left undone. I thank you, Lord, that you are enlarging her territory, and that she is blessed going in and blessed going out. Thank you, Lord, that she is the head and not the tail, above and not beneath. Thank you, Lord, that her vats and barns are overflowing, and that she is entering into a land of milk and honey. Thank you, Lord, that her credit score is A+ and doors are opening up for her in unexpected places. Thank you, Lord, that she will have all of her needs met and she is a lender and not a borrower. Thank you, Lord, that she is a cheerful giver, and she is even investing in her growth. Thank you, Lord, for giving her insight on where to invest for her growth and that she is spending her money wisely. Thank you, Lord, for giving seed to the sower, and multiplying the works of her hands. Thank you, Jesus, that you are opening the windows of heaven upon her, and she will believe who You say she is without doubting or wavering. Thank you, Jesus, that she is the apple of Your eye and with Your strength, she can do all things! Nothing is impossible for You. Lord, I thank you for carrying her on the rest of her journey while on Earth. In Jesus' Name, Amen!

Chapter 23

My Words of Encouragement to You

TransHERmation is an ongoing process throughout our journey with the Lord here on Earth. God's Will is to transform you into the image of His Son. His Will is for you to be made holy and set apart for His purpose. God will give you a glimpse of who you are when He reveals your purpose.

You are created for His purpose and you add value. It is not in your title that you add value, or your degrees, or profession, or job title, marital status, economic status, the house or car you drive, but because you are "You"—you add value. So many people begin to identify themselves with the things that I just named and if one of those things are taken away, they feel they have lost value. Do you know your smile, hug, presence, conversation, and personality add value? I believe God wants us to know who we are before He gives us the promise; He checks our heart's motives before He gives us status in the Kingdom or even status on Earth. He does not want us to identify with the gift more than the gift-giver. He wants us to be able to function in whatever situation we are in. He wants us to trust that when He created us, that He created a masterpiece!

Jesus will test the motives of your heart. How do you act when you don't have any money? How do you act or respond when you have not been publicly identified as a prophet to the nations, but He has revealed it to you? How do you act when you are single and that husband hasn't come along yet? How do you act when you have not gotten that promotion on the job? How do you act when people turn their backs on you? Jesus will test your heart's motives and faithfulness. If you choke up, and don't demonstrate thankfulness and faithfulness to Him in your current state, then He knows that you are not ready for what He has for you.

Are you able to know that you know who you are in Christ, if you have nothing to tangibly show in the physical? I hear in my spirit, *"Who are you trying to impress, Me or man?"*

Paul was content in whatever state he was in. Phil. 4:11-12 states, "I am not saying this because I am in need, for I have learned to be content whatever the circumstances. I know what it is to be in need, and I know what it is to have plenty. I have learned the secret of being content in any and every situation, whether well-fed or hungry, whether living in plenty or want." Being content in your current state is not the same as being stagnant. You are to continue to work towards your goals and purpose until it manifests, but do not surrender to believing you are not valued unless you accomplish those things.

Whatever you are doing right now, you are adding value because you are doing it. Whether it is cleaning floors, washing cars, flipping burgers, ushering or greeting customers—I don't care what it is you are doing. You are adding value because it is "you" doing these things and you are doing them unto the Lord. No matter what you are doing, you have to engage with people; when you do everything as unto the Lord, you are adding value to the people that you are encountering. Colossians 3:23-24, "Whatever you do, work at it with all your heart, as working for the Lord, not for human masters, since you know that you will receive an inheritance from the Lord as a reward. It is the Lord Christ you are serving."

What is your reputation? Do you have favor with God and man because you have a good reputation? This is why it is important to do things as if you are doing it unto the Lord. The Bible tells us that a good reputation is better than silver and gold. Proverbs 22:1, "Choose a good reputation over great riches; being held in high esteem is better than silver and gold." Your reputation is what is going to unlock doors for you and bring you new opportunities.

I shifted to talking about a good reputation because God wants you to know that He values your reputation. He values your attitude. He values your integrity. God even values His own reputation. He delivered the Israelites and pardoned their sin for the sake of His Name. Ezekiel 20:9, "But I didn't do it, for I acted to protect the honor of my name. I would not allow shame to be brought on my name among the surrounding nations who saw me reveal myself by bringing the Israelites out of Egypt." If He did not demonstrate He was God to His chosen ones by delivering them, His name would have been disgraced among the heathen. He valued His Name too much.

You were created in His image. His image is displayed through your unique self. Everybody doesn't sing the same, pray the same, write the same, speak the same or play an instrument in the same way—you get the picture. He is displaying His image in a lot of facets on the Earth. His holiness is demonstrated through your song, your writing, your smile, your hug, your instrument, your speech, your position—no matter what it is. As long as you are walking in holiness in your personality, skills, talents and habits—every part of your life—His image is being displayed. Jesus had twelve disciples and each one had a different personality, but yet He called each one to come and follow Him. God wants you to know that you add value for being who you are; you were fearfully and wonderfully made, and your value is not determined by riches, status or your present state.

When He created you, He created you with great reverence, heartfelt interest, awe and respect. He created you fearfully and He made you wonderfully—unique, set apart and distinctively marvelous. What a revelation. We are to fear Him, but have you ever thought that we are to fear Him by accepting who He created? Accept yourself. He created you to be you! You did not even choose yourself; He chose you. You are His masterpiece. The Bible tells us that the beginning of wisdom is to fear Him—to give Him reverence, respect, be in awe and honor Him.

Well, when He created you, He respected and honored what He created. Speak life into what He created and not death. God is being dishonored when we dishonor ourselves and do not value the uniqueness of who we are. It is flat-out disrespect and dishonor to criticize what God created. Don't you know that you were bought with a price? I Corinthians 6:20, "You were bought at a price. Therefore, honor God with your bodies."

This passage of Scripture is referring to sexual sin, but the principle is not exclusive to sexual sin. Honor God with your mouth. For the Scripture states, "But the things that come out of a person's mouth come from the heart, and these defile them." What is your mouth speaking concerning yourself? Is your mouth saying, "I am not worthy; I can't do this; I'm not capable; I'm unskilled; I'm ugly; I'm poor and will always be poor;" the list can go on and on. What is your mouth speaking? Think about that for a minute. What you are speaking reveals what is in your heart, and those are words of rejection. It's not only time to get healed from rejection of people—but the rejection that you are feeling towards yourself, even God! If you are rejecting yourself, then you are also rejecting God because you are saying what He created is of no use and of no good. When God breathed life into you; He breathed purpose.

This life is a process. Even a diamond is not automatically a diamond; it has to go through the process, through intense heat and pressure. You cannot see the diamond at first, but it is still a diamond that needs to first go through the heat. The heat of refining you; the heat of removing old thinking habits; the heat of removing dead weight and sin out of your life; the heat of removing some relationships and people out of your life. Do not forsake the process—it is only through the process that diamonds are created. If you forsake the process, you will not reach your highest potential. There is a diamond that God wants to produce out of you.

The first step to creating a diamond is a soul cleanse. You should go to the Heavenly Father and seek His face regarding the junk, the sin and residue in your soul. There are some things that we are aware of and others we are not; therefore, we must first go to Him with an honest and open heart. Do not be fearful to go to God and empty yourself before Him. He is a loving daddy that wants the best for you. He is not waiting for you to reveal your heart to Him so He can turn His back on you and forsake you. No. You are His daughter, and He wants to set you free so that you can be effective on the Earth in fulfilling your Kingdom assignment. Beautiful Woman of God, love yourself so that you can love others!

I went through many trials, tribulations and obstacles but God delivered me out of them all, and He will deliver you too! I am married to a wonderful man; and at one time in my life, I thought no one would want me because I had two children by two different fathers—this was spoken into and over my life, and I began to believe it—but God is Faithful and True! I have a God-fearing provider, protector, loving husband that loves me, my sons and granddaughter as his own.

I am a minister and intercessor in the Kingdom of God, and at my home church. At one time, I denied my ability to preach and intercede for people publicly because I was fearful, timid and lacked courage. I looked at all of my inabilities instead of the One that Created and called me—but God, the Faithful One, brought it about. I now also minister to the lost in jail and at a homeless shelter for women. I never thought that I would have the courage to minister and encourage other women.

It was prophesied to me on many occasions that I would write a book, and I never knew how or where to start. But I obeyed God and now I am writing a book. I am also doing live Periscope videos, and that took the act of God too because I doubted myself out of fear, having no platform, and I lacked confidence in what Jesus could do through me.

I decided to trust God and step out and face fear head on. Now, I do Periscopes regularly, and I am more comfortable with it than when I first started. Not only that, I have tapped into my entrepreneurial side by writing a book, selling TransHERmation T-shirts, selling jewelry on the side, and I am currently working on a TransHERmation Empowerment Coaching program for women that have been through some things, that have a dream; and are ready to get empowered. The keyword ladies, is READY to be empowered. Be ready to be empowered and transformed.

I commission you to begin to take the time right now to open yourself up before God and ask Him to show you who He created you to be. Ask Him to reveal His calling on your life, knowing that He is faithful to complete the work He has begun.

In all my prayers for all of you, I always pray with joy
because of your partnership in the gospel
from the first day until now,
being confident of this,
that he who began a good work in you
will carry it on to completion
until the day of Christ Jesus.
Philippians 1:4-6

Acknowledgements

I first want to give thanks and acknowledge my Lord and personal Savior, Jesus Christ. It was through Him that TransHERmation was first birthed. I want to give thanks to my husband and best friend, Dwayne Kelly, for being my number one supporter and rock through writing this book; he has made this journey a lot easier. My sons, DeeVon Carmouche and Adrian Clark, for being my reason to keep pushing, even when I wanted to throw in the towel. My granddaughter, Azah Clark, for giving me a reason to leave a legacy someday. My mom, Cynthia Little, for being my second best friend, fan, follower and supporter. Thank you to my children, Damonte Thomas and Kornique Geter. Thank you to my family, church family—New Harvest Christian Center, and Pastors Ivan and Tina Lee, Freedom Faith Worship Center, and to my friends that have supported me through encouraging words, prophetic words, prayers, and financial support.

A special thank you to my friends, Denise Ruffin and Kenneth McGee, for their sponsorship support of this book. A special thank you to my friend and sister in Christ, Patrice Burrell, for her sponsorship support, prayers and encouragement. A special thank you to my cousins, Tommie and Margaret Kirk, owners of Massage Green Spa in Battle Creek and Kalamazoo, MI, for their sponsorship support and prayers. A special thank you to my friends and family in Christ, Dr. Michael and LaTisha Glass, owners of Glass Family Dental.

Thank you to Tiffany Smith, for encouraging me to get this book done sooner than later. Thank you to my spiritual grandmother, Ophelia Hoskins, for always being a listening ear and providing sound wisdom through my journey. Thank you to my spiritual mother, Jarry Turner, for always warring on my behalf.

Thank you to Robmieka Gibson and Victoria Thompson; I appreciate the both of you for helping me with the planning of my launch. Thank you to everyone that has purchased this book; I appreciate your support!

About the Author

Minster Lakeea Kelly ultimately loves her family, people and ministry! She dedicates her life to the Lord and stands on the Scripture that states, "Do to others as you would have them do to you." This is the Golden Rule that Minister Lakeea lives by.

A native of Battle Creek, MI, Minister Lakeea is also an active member of New Harvest Christian Center, under Pastors Ivan and Tina Lee. She serves on the Ministerial and Outreach Team by ministering at the local jail and women's shelter. Minister Lakeea accepted Jesus Christ in her life at the age of nine, again at twelve, and decided to live sold out for the Lord at the age of twenty-nine.

In 2006, Minister Lakeea obtained a bachelor's degree in Family Life Education from Spring Arbor University, and studied Counseling Psychology at Western Michigan University. Today, she works as an Equal Employment Opportunity Manager at the Battle Creek Veterans Affairs Medical Center in Battle Creek, and has served as a mentor and coach for other staff.

Minster Lakeea enjoys being a mentor and coach to young ladies by empowering them through encouragement, godly counsel, the Word of God and prayer. She is a mentor for Tenacious G.E.M.S. (Girls Empowerment and Mentoring Services) for girls and young women ages 12 – 25, under its founder Ms. Timeya Gray. Her passion for the lives of others is consistently demonstrated in her family, church and community.

Minister Lakeea is a new and rising author, entrepreneur and certified coach. She loves to empower, impart and build people up to become what God has called them to be. Additionally, she carries a mantle of intercession, with a passion for the gospel of Jesus Christ, and a desire to see souls saved, healed and delivered. She is married to Elder Dwayne Kelly, and they have been blessed with four children and three grandchildren.